CHARTING
YOUR COURSE...
BY GOD'S DREAM
IN YOUR HEART

CHARTING
YOUR COURSE...
BY GOD'S DREAM
IN YOUR HEART

Robert Tilton Ministries
Dallas, Texas

All of our books are part of our free worldwide Gospel Literature Crusade. If you'd like to make a donation to help spread the Gospel of Jesus Christ, please send it to the address below.

Charting Your Course by God's Dream in Your Heart
ISBN 0-914307-88-6
(Formerly ISBN 0-89274-404-9 and ISBN 0-914307-11-8)
Copyright © 1990 by Robert Tilton Ministries
First Printing, October 1990

Published by Robert Tilton Ministries
P. O. Box 819000, Dallas, Texas 75381-9000
(Canadian Address:
P. O. Box 4900, Vancouver, British Columbia, V6B 4A6)
Printed in the United States of America
All Rights Reserved
No Reproduction Without Permission
Editor: Kathryn P. Ingley

Contents

Before any wise sailor leaves port, he charts the course to his destination. You shouldn't do any less in your life.

Contents

Preface

"I will not be satisfied with being a sailboat, drifting around. I will...chart my course in the sea of life."

Mary was one of the wealthiest women in Houston, Texas, and she counted many national leaders among her friends. But she wasn't always wealthy and her story did not start out beautiful.

When she was 40, Mary's husband divorced her and left her with four children. She had no way of earning an income, and her landlord evicted them. Still she wrote this:

"I will rise again. I am 40 years old, divorced and broke. My four children and I have just been evicted from our apartment. I thought my world had come to an end. I have never been so depressed, so lonely, so frightened. I do not understand life today. I am the sole support of four children and myself. I am not going to cry anymore, though. This is only a temporary situation, because the things which are seen in the natural are temporary.

"I have been happy before. I will be happy again. Today is the first day of the rest of my life. I will set a good example for my children. I am going to take them to church and teach them about God. I will motivate them and inspire them. I will be the best mother in the world.

"I will be somebody someday. Someday kings, queens, heads of state, and even presidents and other important people will ask my advice and listen to me.

"I will not let anyone or anything limit me. I will not be satisfied with being a sailboat out in the sea, drifting around. I will...chart my course in the sea of life.

"There will be obstacles. There will be some setbacks. There may be some detours, but I refuse to let them destroy me. It will not be easy, but I am going to make it. I will win the battle. I will win the war.

"I will turn this loss into a cornerstone for my life, and I will rebuild again. I will succeed. I will keep going. I will not look back. I have many obligations, and my children are depending on me. With God's help, I will rise again!"

Mary refused to give up, even when everything seemed to be against her. She did not look back, but she looked forward and God gave her a new direction. She had a dream, and she purposed in her heart to bring that dream into reality.

> A good man out of the good treasure of the heart bringeth forth good things.
>
> Matthew 12:35

She prophesied her dream and then, with much labor, brought her prophecy to pass. She wrote her own ticket with God.

> My heart is inditing a good matter: I speak of the things which I have made touching the king: my tongue is the pen of a ready writer.
>
> Psalm 45:1

Perhaps your life, like Mary's, has fallen apart and you need to start over. Or, perhaps, you are young and just starting out. The direction you go depends on what you see in your dreams. I am asking God to let this book open your eyes so that you can dream. Then I am asking God to motivate you to act on those dreams.

In this book, I am going to show you how to chart your course through life by the dreams God has placed in your heart. First I will show you how to select the right dream and start with it. Then I will show you how to plan your life, how to run with your dream, how to chart your course and decree your destiny. If you will stay with me through the entire book, you will learn how to take charge of your life and use your dreams to turn it around.

Let's Pray

Father, I give You all the glory and all the praise because I know that except You build the house (life), we labor in vain.[1]

I pray that every believer reading this book will understand how to act upon his dreams and see them become realities.

I thank You for letting us dream, imagine, and think, and I thank You for giving us Your creativity in our spirits. I thank You that You have not left us when we became frustrated, but have helped us to see our dreams come to pass. God, I believe it is You Who gives these dreams to us so that we can see them realized in our lives.

Father, You see every person that is reading this book and I believe that You will reveal Jesus to them in signs, wonders, and miracles. I believe You for these things. I believe that as the Word goes forth from this book, miracles will take place, and eyes will be opened.

Father, we thank You, in Jesus' name. Amen.

---

[1]Psalm 127:1

1

Start with Your Dream

God's plan for your life is often hidden in your dreams, and you can see it only by using His spiritual microscope.

Everyone has dreams—dreams which they would like to accomplish in their lifetime. But only a few chart a course for their lives according to those dreams. Perhaps others do not realize that their dreams might be God's plan for their lives.

When I say dreams, I am not talking about those images that fill your mind during sleep, nor the wild fantasies or hopes that you conjure up when you daydream. I'm talking about the deep-seated aspirations and ambitions that fill your heart and thoughts and won't leave you alone.

Madeline Manning Mims had a dream of getting out of the ghettos in Cleveland and making something of herself. Everyone she shared her dream with told her she could not do this because everything was against her. But she would not give up her dream.

Then after making Jesus Christ her Savior and Lord, Madeline found she could run. She saw running as her ticket out of the ghettos. Jesus inspired her to overcome every obstacle, and, in 1968, she won an Olympic Gold Medal for setting a new world record on the 800-meter run. Madeline learned that her dream was from God and was His plan for her life.

> Now unto him that is able to do exceeding abundantly above all that we ask or think, according to the POWER THAT WORKETH IN US.   Ephesians 3:20

God created you to dream, and, in fact, He inspires your dreams. Since the word "inspire" means *to blow on or breathe upon; to be motivated and guided by divine influence*, you could say that your dreams are *God breathed*, which means they are given by the Holy Spirit. **That dream in your heart is an inspired idea from God.**

Marte and I came to Dallas because God inspired our thoughts by a scripture in Proverbs:

> Roll your works [what you are involved in]
> upon the Lord—commit and trust them wholly
> to Him; [He will cause your thoughts to
> become agreeable to His will, and] so shall
> your plans be established and succeed.
>   Proverbs 16:3 (AMP)

He had told us to start a family church, and that
commission became a dream that consumed us
and would not leave us alone. But we waited
before Him until He told us to come to Farmers
Branch in north Dallas. The scripture in Proverbs
caused us to stretch our faith and to obey His
instructions, step by step. Because of our obedience, Word of Faith Family Church and Robert
Tilton Ministries are now involved in international
ministry and influencing thousands of lives each
day.

Have you ever noticed that when you are
reading your Bible, suddenly something will
stand out to you that you had not seen before?
That is the Spirit of God illuminating your
understanding and revealing things to you. God
gives you this inspired understanding to help you
learn to walk by the principles in His Word.[2]

> But there is a spirit in man: and the inspira-
> tion of the Almighty giveth them under-
> standing.   Job 32:8

**You can use your dreams to recognize God's
plan for your life.** God had a dream, in the
beginning, when He created the heavens and the
earth.[3] This dream became God's master plan, His

[2] I Corinthians 2:9,10   [3] Genesis 1:1

blueprint, for man and everything on the earth. Genesis tells us that God spoke His plan into existence.

> And God said, Let there be light: and there
> was light.   Genesis 1:3

Later, He inspired others to write His words so that people could build their lives by them.[4] The Bible, that written record of God's words, is His master plan for your future. When you believe and act upon its principles, the things He recorded will come to pass.

You see, God preprogrammed His plan for your life in the same way that He placed certain characteristics in each seed to give it the ability to develop into a new plant just like the mother plant.

> And God said, Let the earth bring forth grass,
> the herb yielding seed, and the fruit tree
> yielding fruit after his kind, *whose seed is in
> itself*, upon the earth: and it was so.
>   Genesis 1:11

I looked up the word preprogrammed and found that it comes from the Greek word *prographein* which means *to set forth as a public notice; to write forth*. The word "preprogrammed" means *something that has been programmed beforehand, or recorded in advance*. A computer's software contains its prerecorded programs, but both software and hardware are needed to run these programs.

[4]II Timothy 3:16

The Bible was preprogrammed to play back God's plan for your eternal life, prosperity, health, and happiness. It is God's software, and you are His hardware. And only when you follow God's Word, will His plan germinate in you and produce a healthy life.

God's plan for your life is often hidden in your dreams, and you can see it only by using His spiritual microscope called the "eye of faith."

> While we look not at the things which are seen, but at the things which are not seen: for the things which are seen are temporal; but the things which are not seen are eternal.
>
> II Corinthians 4:18

Your dream, like a seed, has been preprogrammed to mature into reality. But it can lie there and never release what is inside it if it is not properly planted, watered, and cultivated. When you take that dream and plant it by faith and nurture it on God's principles, it will blossom into a wondrous reality.

If you will allow Him, God will work with your dreams. It is easy to become frustrated when your dream does not become a reality immediately, but if your dream is based on God's Word, your faith will bring it into reality.

Success always breeds more success. And the bigger things you do, the bigger things you can do. By understanding and using what God's Word says about success, you can do bigger things. Many people are ignorant of this fact, but a few are waking up to the hopes and dreams in them.

When Jesus gave believers the keys of the kingdom, He gave them the authority to run His program, His plan, and to loose what was in the earth so that they could fulfill their dreams.

> And I will give unto thee the keys of the kingdom of heaven: and whatsoever thou shalt bind on earth shall be bound in heaven: and whatsoever thou shalt loose on earth shall be loosed in heaven.   Matthew 16:19

Examine your dreams by God's Word and select a big one, one that is dear to you but realistic. That's what Mary Kay of Dallas, Texas, did. She married during World War II and began raising a family. At the close of the war, her husband divorced her and left her and their children with no financial support.

Since she didn't have a profession, she began to support herself by selling products door-to-door. But after working hard for three weeks, she found that her income averaged only seven dollars a week.

One day she sat on the back row at a sales meeting and watched one of the women crowned queen for the year because she had sold the most products. She thought, "I'm going to be crowned, too," and one year later the crown was placed on her head.

This achievement might not have been important to anyone else, but it was to Mary Kay.

It was the first step toward achieving her dream. After she was crowned queen of sales, she began to dream of starting her own cosmetic line—Mary Kay Cosmetics.

Today, she owns one of the largest cosmetic companies in the world. Mary Kay Cosmetics does over two hundred million dollars worth of business a year, and she has over one hundred fifty thousand women working for her as independent consultants. But it all started with her dream.

Because of her dream, Mary Kay has been able to help thousands of women succeed. She takes beaten-down women, lifts them up and lets them know they are someone special. She talks to them, loves them, and encourages them.

When asked about her dream Mary Kay said, "I started Mary Kay Cosmetics to give other women the opportunity I felt I had been denied. I wanted to give women the opportunity to go as far as their abilities would take them, and to be the very best they could.

"I wanted to give women a chance to know they are wonderful and special. I wanted to give them the opportunity to know they could succeed beyond their wildest dreams. Now, my dream has become a wonderful reality.

"If you will put God first and let Him be the dominating force in your life, keep your family second as it should be, and your job in third place, you will be successful. I've proved that it works."

Mary Kay planned her life and business according to the dream in her heart. Many people fail to do that; they plan all sorts of other things, but somehow they don't see the importance of planning their lives.

They remind me of airplanes. I've had to spend a lot of time around airplanes and have become fascinated with them, especially since I've realized that people can be a lot like them. Let's look at the similarities. Airplanes were made to fly. Some were made to travel fast; others, slow; and some are jets. But some are just parked in a hangar and never get out. Others get up in the sky and fly in circles. A few even crash. Some come right back to where they started and never get where they wanted to go. But a few take off, climb high above the clouds and really soar; they explore the world and go wherever they wish. They do what they were designed to do—they fly.

People are the same. Too many of us are parked in hangars, or are flying in circles, or never getting anywhere. We were designed to dream and to fulfill those dreams. That's what this book is all about; I want to get you out of your hangar, and fill you up with the fuel of the Holy Spirit, and help you take off. I want to show you how to chart your course according to the dreams in your heart and the principles in God's Word.

Some people try to fly by sight. They get up in the air and become frightened. All they see are clouds, and no ground. They become disoriented and begin to think all kinds of strange things: they are flying straight up or straight down. They are having a hard time because they have never learned to use the instruments: God's Word and the power and anointing of the Holy Spirit.

You don't have to be like those people because in the next chapter, I'm going to show you how to make your plan and how to use your instruments.

2

Make a Plan for Your Life

A dream without a plan is like a ship without a rudder or a compass: it has no purposeful direction.

Adream must have a plan behind it to be successful. Hard work is not enough. Many people work hard but because they fail to plan, their dreams remain only dreams. If you want to succeed, you must think seriously about your dream and plan for it to come true. God's Word instructs us to make such a plan and to make it strong through common sense.

> Any enterprise is built by wise planning, be-
> comes strong through common sense, and
> profits wonderfully by keeping abreast of the
> facts.   Proverbs 24:3-4 (TLB)

Before any wise sailor leaves port, he charts the course to his destination. A sailor's chart is a group of facts set up to form a diagram or a map. It maps out in detail the coastlines, water depths and even special weather data. It may also contain other information that is needed by the ship's navigator to get his ship to its destination.

That's the kind of plan you should make for your life—one that covers all the adventures and dangers. The prophet Habakkuk records God's command to write your plan in detail.

> And the Lord answered me, and said, Write
> the vision, and make it plain upon tables, that
> he may run that readeth it.
>   Habakkuk 2:2

Here's what you should write:

- your dream
- your plan for making it a reality, including all the steps necessary to reach your goal
- your hopes
- your expectations, what you are believing God for this year

Of course, it will take some time to write all of these things in detail, but you are not wasting time; you are focusing your thinking on your dream. Time spent doing this charting will save you much grief and time later on.

When I was a mechanical designer, I designed a conveyor for a major corporation and drew blueprints for the workmen to use in cutting a hole in an expensive wall for its installation. My design for the conveyor was inspired, but I had to do the tedious work of drawing the blueprint to bring it to reality. The conveyor belt fit perfectly because the blueprints I had drawn up were accurate.

When you plan something in advance you must sit down and think, and this usually requires some effort. But without these plans, your dream will never materialize.

In addition to thinking about and planning your dream in detail, you need to purpose to make your dream a reality. You could write all the details and yet not act on your dream. To "purpose" means *to resolve to perform or accomplish something*. That means making a commitment; that means sticking with your plan until it succeeds; that means not giving up regardless of circumstances or criticisms.

Listening to the Spirit of God is the second step in making a blueprint, or chart, for your life. Many inspired ideas that could enrich the world may be in you, but first they must get out. By identifying your dream, planning, acting with purpose, and listening to the Spirit of God, you can bring these inspired ideas and dreams into reality.

God may have placed in you ideas for things not yet known, or heard, or seen. These ideas could include:

- business opportunities
- songs
- designs for houses
- books or plays
- paintings

The list could go on and on. But if you will take your idea and lay it before the Lord, He will direct you and show you how to bring it into reality. But the secret is in the listening. You may listen to God in many ways, but I want to share with you a few ways that Marte and I have learned to listen to Him.

Part of listening to God is submitting all your "bitter waters" to Him. The children of Israel would have died of thirst in the wilderness of Shur if Moses had not told God about the bitter waters and been sensitive to God's voice.[5]

> Then Moses led the people of Israel on from the Red Sea, and they moved out into the wilderness of Shur and were three days without water.
>
> Arriving at Marah, they couldn't drink the water because it was bitter (that is why the place was called Marah, meaning "bitter").
>
> Then the people turned against Moses. "Must we die of thirst?" they demanded.
>
> Moses pleaded with the Lord to help them, and the Lord showed him a tree to throw into the water, and the water became sweet.

[5]Exodus 15:22-24

> It was there at Marah that the Lord laid before them the following conditions, to test their commitment to him:
>
> If you will listen to the voice of the Lord your God, and obey it, and do what is right, then I will not make you suffer the diseases I sent on the Egyptians, for I am the Lord who heals you.   Exodus 15:22-26 (TLB)

The tree that Moses threw into the waters was a symbol of Calvary. We all find bitter waters in life, but by listening to God's Spirit we learn that Jesus, who hung on the tree at Calvary, makes bitter waters sweet. Not only does He sweeten the waters, but He gives us living water to drink which will quench our thirst throughout eternity.[6]

Another part of listening to God is looking for the oasis of God's guidance and presence. Immediately after the experience of the bitter waters, the children of Israel found an oasis at Elim—a place of abundant water and shade to shield them from the heat of the sun.

> And they came to Elim where there were twelve springs and seventy palm trees; and they camped there beside the springs.
>   Exodus 15:27 (TLB)

An "oasis" is *a fertile green spot of land surrounded by a desert or waste*. It can also mean *a small place preserved from surrounding unpleasantness*. By living in the oasis of God's presence, you will have peace and happiness in the midst of every strenuous difficulty, and can expect—and receive—God's guidance.

[6]John 4:13-14

Submitting your plans to God is also part of listening to God. Marte and I expect to see God's blessings and guidance in our lives. We expect to see our dreams succeed because we have submitted all our plans and dreams to the will of God, and we live constantly in His presence.

As long as Adam and Eve were submissive to God's will, they had abundant life and authority.

> And God said, Let us make man in our image, after our likeness: and *let them have dominion* over the fish of the sea, and over the fowl of the air, and over the cattle, and over all the earth, and over every creeping thing that creepeth upon the earth.
> And God blessed them, and God said unto them, Be fruitful, and multiply, and replenish the earth, and subdue it: and *have dominion* over the fish of the sea, and over the fowl of the air, and over every living thing that moveth upon the earth.   Genesis 1:26, 28

Although God created man to rule the earth, subdue it, and cause it to yield fruit,[7] man's lack of submission and disobedience caused him to lose this authority.

> Now the serpent was more subtle than any beast of the field which the Lord God had made. And he said unto the woman, Yea, hath God said, Ye shall not eat of every tree of the garden?
> For God doth know that in the day ye eat thereof, then your eyes shall be opened, and ye shall be as gods, knowing good and evil.

[7]Genesis 2:15

> And when the woman saw that the tree
> was good for food, and that it was pleasant to
> the eyes, and a tree to be desired to make one
> wise, she took of the fruit thereof, and did eat,
> and gave also unto her husband with her; and
> he did eat. Genesis 3:1, 5-6

As a consequence of man's sin, death entered the human race. (Sickness is death in operation.) Man died both spiritually and physically,[8] and his natural senses and the information collected through these senses ruled him. Sin left him naked, fearful and vulnerable to Satan's influence. "Naked" means *to be without covering; to be stripped or to be defenseless or vulnerable*. When Adam and Eve refused to submit to God's instructions, they allowed Satan to master them and take away their authority and dominion. They became defenseless against the surrounding adverse circumstances.

> And the eyes of them both were opened, and
> they knew that they were naked; and they
> sewed fig leaves together, and made them-
> selves aprons.
> And they heard the voice of the Lord God
> walking in the garden in the cool of the day;
> and Adam and his wife hid themselves from
> the presence of the Lord God amongst the
> trees of the garden.
> And he said, I heard thy voice in the gar-
> den, and I was afraid, because I was naked;
> and I hid myself. Genesis 3:7-8, 10

Adam's fall (disobedience, rebellion, and sin) gave Satan dominion, but Jesus Christ, the last

[8]Genesis 2:17

Adam, restored mankind back to a right relationship (righteousness) with God. Once again we
can say, "Abba Father."

> For if by one man's offence death reigned by
> one; much more they which receive abundance
> of grace and of the gift of righteousness shall
> reign in life by one, Jesus Christ.
> For as by one man's disobedience many
> were made sinners, so by the obedience of one
> shall many be made righteous.
>
> Romans 5:17, 19

**The next step, then, in charting your life is
to take authority over circumstances.** The word
"circumstance" comes from the Latin *circumstare*
which means *to stand around*. This gives "circumstance" the meaning of *the condition or facet
surrounding an event or having some bearing on
it*. In other words, circumstances are the things
and situations surrounding you.

You can take authority over circumstances
when you are righteous, when you are *in right
standing with God*, and are walking uprightly.
The Spirit of life in Jesus makes you free from
the law of sin and death.

> For the law of the Spirit of life in Christ Jesus
> hath made me free from the law of sin and
> death.   Romans 8:2

The blood of Jesus frees you from sin. Because
of your right relationship with the Father, God
has restored to you the authority to reign over
all your circumstances and adversities.

God will withhold no good thing from you when you walk uprightly.[9] You will have abundant life, spiritual victory, good health and prosperity. Release your faith and you can overcome all circumstances:

- sickness
- disease
- failing finances
- failing business
- failing marriage

In my files I have the testimony of a woman who had a skin disease which her doctors said was incurable. She could not wash her face with water or wear any makeup, and exposure to the wind would cause her skin to crack and bleed.

Her face became so disfigured that people could not bear to look at her. Her husband left her and her family kicked her out on to the street, so she came to live in Dallas. While here, she began watching my daily television program, *Success-N-Life*, and heard my wife, Marte, teach on the name of Jesus and the authority that believers have in His name. This woman believed what Marte taught, and obeyed when I asked those who needed prayer to lay their hands on the television screen.

Instantly, as she placed her hand on the screen, she felt a twitch in her cheek and reached up to touch it. She found her skin soft for the first time in years. Jesus not only took her skin

[9]Psalm 84:11

disease away, but He restored her skin.

This woman got her miracle because she heard the truth, believed and had faith to take authority over the circumstances of her incurable disease. God's Word released health instead of sickness, and her dream became a reality.

God wants to make your dream a reality too. He can do anything you will give Him the opportunity to do. God can do big things or little things,[10] because He knows no limit. That's the kind of God He is. He will withhold no good thing from you when you walk uprightly.

> For the Lord God is a sun and shield: the Lord will give grace and glory: no good thing will he withhold from them that walk uprightly.
> Psalm 84:11

You were not created for sickness, hurt, or heartbreak, but for eternal life, life worth living and getting excited about. The word "eternal" means *without beginning or end; timeless; without interruption*. Eternal life, then, is *a life that cannot be measured*. When you have eternal life, you have so much life that its length, height, depth, or width cannot be measured. God created you for this type of life.

But you must follow your spirit, not your senses. The carnal mind, which is controlled by the senses, sees only lack, death, sickness, and failure. "To be carnal minded is death."[11] Carnal-minded people are limited by what they can perceive through their senses, and often they see only failure.

[10] I Samuel 14:6 [11] Romans 8:6

"To be spiritually minded is life and peace,"[12] and this is the law of abundance. A spiritual-minded person, who is no longer a slave to his senses but who is controlled by the Holy Spirit, can do all things[13] because he has:

- Confidence—I can make it!
- Determination—I can do it!
- Success—I can overcome!

Instead of being overcome by life, he overcomes. Instead of allowing circumstances to rule him, he rules them. Instead of allowing adversities to enslave him, he conquers them. As God's Word renews his mind, he wants to do the good, accep-table, and the perfect will of God.[14]

And that includes learning to **trust God to fulfill your desires.** Nothing is too hard for God, nor can He be limited, except by your unbelief. Simple childlike faith and trust are all that is necessary.

The prophet's widow in II Kings 4 did not realize that she had all that she needed, and because of this lack of knowledge, she almost lost her sons.

> Now there cried a certain woman of the wives of the sons of the prophets unto Elisha, say-ing, Thy servant my husband is dead; and thou knowest that thy servant did fear the Lord: and the creditor is come to take unto him my two sons to be bondmen.   II Kings 4:1

She was in terrible circumstances. Her creditors threatened to take her two sons and sell

---

[12]Romans 8:6 [13]Philippians 4:13 [14]Romans 12:2

them into slavery in payment of her debt. Frustrated, worried and heartsick, she saw no way of escape. She was surrounded—*circumstanced*—and could not see above the mountains of trouble.

But God sent a prophet to her. This woman did not think she had anything that would help her solve her problem, but she did not see what the prophet Elisha saw. The very thing she thought too insignificant, her little pot of oil, was what God used. Elisha told her to get all the vessels she could find and start pouring from her little pot of oil.

> And Elisha said unto her, What shall I do for thee? tell me, what hast thou in the house? And she said, Thine handmaid hath not any thing in the house, save a pot of oil.
> Then he said, Go, borrow thee vessels abroad of all thy neighbours, even empty vessels; borrow not a few.
> And when thou art come in, thou shalt shut the door upon thee and upon thy sons, and shalt pour out into all those vessels, and thou shalt set aside that which is full.
> So she went from him, and shut the door upon her and upon her sons, who brought the vessels to her; and she poured out.
> And it came to pass, when the vessels were full, that she said unto her son, Bring me yet a vessel. And he said unto her, There is not a vessel more. And the oil stayed.
> Then she came and told the man of God. And he said, Go, sell the oil, and pay thy debt, and live thou and thy children of the rest.
>   II Kings 4:2-7

Your dreams and resources may also seem insignificant, but God will use what you have to deliver and prosper you. All He wants is for you to believe His Word and trust Him to fulfill your desires. Many people go for years waiting for a big idea or dream when they already have all they need to fulfill their dreams.

But you must start where you are, with what you have. Don't wait for the perfect situation. There has never been a day like today. I believe the Spirit of God wants to give people who are faithful in the small things inventions that will bring them worldwide recognition and prominence. I believe God is going to help Christians do things that will boggle the mind and stagger the imagination. This is why you need to start with what you have and not wait for the perfect situation or dream.

An acorn may look insignificant, but God preprogrammed it to grow into a mighty oak tree—when planted and nourished. The same thing happens when you mix the seed of God's Word with faith—it comes alive and grows mighty within you.

A few years ago, a pastor told me the story of a new convert in his church who needed a job, but he had no education or training.

"What can you do?" the pastor asked.

"I can't do anything," the man replied. "The only work I ever did was washing cars at a service station."

"Then we are going to make you into a super-duper executive car washer," the pastor said. "First, we need to have a brochure printed for you, and then you are going to become a custom car wash specialist."

The man dressed himself in brand-new khaki clothes, as his pastor instructed, and went, with his brochures, to knock on the doors of a nearby office building. He got more business than he could handle. He would peddle his bicycle over to pick up a car, and drive it to his house to wash. Afterwards, he drove it back and picked up another car.

Soon he had more cars than he could wash in one day, so he hired some high school students to help him. Finally, his business grew large enough for him to buy a car wash that had gone out of business. He has more money now than he knows what to do with. Why? Because he started with what he could do—wash cars—and worked diligently with it. He planted one little idea and nourished it.

Giving in expectation of God's blessings on your dream is another way of nourishing an idea. Not long ago a woman who had never made over $700 dollars a month before God became her senior partner wrote me a letter.

"Brother Tilton," she wrote, "I have been listening to you talk about giving. At first I was turned off, but then I began listening to what you were saying and I heard God talking to me. I found that money was a part of me and that if I wanted to receive God's blessings, I had to make room for God in my house by giving.

"You challenged me to give $100. I scarcely had that much, but I gave it and believed God, like you said, for my return.

"Soon after this, Brother Tilton, I was driving down the freeway when suddenly the idea came into my spirit to buy a van and daily bus the children in my neighborhood to school. I knew this was from God, so I bought the van and started bussing the children. Now I am clearing $500 a week."

> Be not deceived; God is not mocked: for what-
> soever a man soweth, that shall he also reap.
> Galatians 6:7

The amount you sow determines what you receive or earn from your labors. This woman reaped her miracle because she released her faith in giving.

Marte and I decreed years ago, when we were eating beans and cornbread, that we would be paymasters for God. And we are. We believe in the law of sowing and reaping. The world said we would never make it, but we said, through Jesus Christ we could do all things.[15]

But even planting and nourishing an idea will not work unless you're willing to get out of your box. Gunder Birkeland, who died in

---

[15]Philippians 4:13

January 1976, at 90, was one of the wealthiest men in Seattle. Yet as a child it looked like he would never amount to much.

Gunder Birkeland was born in Norway around 1886. When he was two years old, he contracted polio and his legs shriveled up and wouldn't work. The doctors knew little about treating polio and were not able to help. So his parents put him in a wooden box which they pulled around with a rope. In the winter, they added ski runners to it, and in the summer, wheels.

Over the years Gunder would hear people talking about him. "He won't last long." "He'll probably die." "He won't ever amount to much." "He'll never walk." Can you imagine hearing words of death being spoken over you day after day? Can you imagine watching others walk by while you sat in a box?

One day, when he was seven years old, his parents sat him in front of a mirror. As he looked at himself, he had a vision in which he was standing on his feet like a normal man.

After that, every day Gunder would rock back and forth until the box would tip over. If his parents caught him doing this, they would spank him and put him back in his box. But as soon as they left he would begin rocking again, trying to get out of his box.

Gunder saw himself walking like everyone else, and often exclaimed, "I'm getting out of this box!" And he got out.

Later, he learned to crawl, and then to get up on his legs. After much hard work, he learned to walk—something people thought he could never do.

Gunder became one of the ten wealthiest men in Seattle. (The Seattle Space Needle was built on his property.) In his twilight years, he said, "I realized that I did not have to stay in that box. My mission in life is to tell people this: You don't have to stay in the box either. You can get out. You can become what you see in your spirit and in your dream. And you can obtain. You can abound in this life. You can get out of the box. You don't have to be surrounded by adversity or circumstances. You can get out of your box."

Gunder had a vision, and that vision got him out of his box. What he saw in his spirit became his. Mary Kay, the car wash executive, and the prophet's widow all got out of their boxes when they charted their lives by the dreams God had placed in their hearts and obeyed what He told them to do.

Satan is still putting people in boxes by telling them that they will never:

- amount to anything
- do anything
- have any money

- be healed
- have a decent marriage

In the past, some people have said, "Robert Tilton will never amount to much." "He will leave the ministry in two years." More than sixteen years have passed and Marte and I are still in the ministry, and are doing more than we have ever done. We dreamt that we could get out of our box, and we got out.

You too, will get out of your box if you believe. So go ahead and chart your life by the dream in your heart, and God will direct your steps. Your dream will become powerful as you act on it. As part of the Body of Jesus Christ, you have been programmed to succeed.

> If God be for us, who can be against us?
> Romans 8:31

So stick with your dream and don't quit. Believe that you will get out of your box. Don't let the devil zap you with fear. Stay in the Word of God and listen constantly to His Spirit. And, remember, if you find a few closed doors, simply regroup and try again! So what if you make a mistake. Simply turn the mistake into a retake and go forward again.

3

Clarify Your Vision

*Your godly desire, like a vision, gives you
the ability to see beyond what is and to
bring about what should be.*

You can run with your dream when you
know where you are going, when you
clarify your vision. You won't be like the
airplane that takes off and flies in circles over the
field and then lands, going nowhere and
accomplishing nothing. Your dream will direct
where you go; it will determine your direction
and your goals. In this chapter, I want to show
you how to clarify your vision.

First, recognize your dream as your purpose of being. During the first 21 years of my life I was not sure where I was going. Many times I wondered why I had been born, and what I was supposed to be doing. I had many talents and interests, but I never felt that any of them was my purpose for living.

Then Marte and I found the answers to the questions in our lives when some young people came to share Christ with us. At that time Jesus spoke to my spirit and said, "I have called you to be a minister of My Gospel. I have called you to be a fisher of men." In that split second of time I knew my purpose in life was to be a soul winner, a fisher of men, a minister of the Gospel.

Prior to that day, I had laughed at preachers and imitated them while sitting at the bar drinking beer with my buddies. But in a split second of time, I found Christ and discovered my reason for living and my purpose in life; I was transformed and fulfilled.

You, too, have a purpose on this earth. There is a reason for your being alive. You have a calling. There is a place for you in God's creation that no one else can fill. The word "purpose" is defined as *a reason for which something exists, a goal or an aim, the object toward which one strives*. Your dream defines your reason for existing and gives you the key to your future.

A "dream" is defined as: *a fond hope; a*

strong aspiration or desire; an anticipation of a positive expectation. You see, your dream not only gives you a hope and an expectation for your future, but acting on it brings you the fulfillment you long for.

Unfortunately, some people never acknowledge their dreams and never find the purpose for their being. Satan steals their dreams. And a few cannot see any reason to go on living so they commit suicide.

Perhaps Satan has been doing the same to you—trying to steal, kill, and destroy your dreams. That's what Jesus said Satan would try to do. But Jesus not only places within you His dream for your life, but also the power of the Holy Spirit to enable you to fulfill it. When I found Christ, I discovered my reason for being and my purpose in life. You will too.

Once you know your purpose, you can set your goals which are simply an outgrowth of your commitment to your dream; you are determined to succeed, to win, so you make a list of the steps necessary to win, to fulfill your dream, and you think about and act on them constantly. They are the first things you think about in the morning and the last thoughts you have at night. You know exactly what you want and what it takes to get it.

We get what we think about; we achieve what we work toward. That's why someone said,

"Be choosy, therefore, what you set your heart upon. For if you want it strongly enough, you'll get it."

If you have a goal that is in agreement with the Word of God and that is worthy of you as a person, never waver from it. Draw joy and excitement from it and faithfully move toward it. As it nears, start thinking ahead to the next step. That's how Marte and I built this ministry.

Some people have tried to analyze the reason for the success of the Word of Faith Family Church. One of these was a nationally known evangelist who asked, "Bob, what do you think has done the most in helping Word of Faith become successful in the work of God?"

After much thought I said, "We are accomplishing things for God because we know where we are going! We have a dream, a vision from Him and we have purposed to fulfill that for Him. We know where we are going. We have a vision and a direction with purpose."

Success did not happen instantly, but it was like climbing a staircase, each step led to the step ahead. This has helped us to see where we are going.

If you never waver from your goals then you will not lose your purpose for living. That is the key to your vision and future. When you can see your dream, when you can have hope, when you see your reason for living, then you can move with purposeful action—action with a purpose.

But until you settle on a purpose, you may have lots of action but still get nowhere. Like that airplane circling aimlessly in the sky, you have no destination. If you really want to know what your purpose is, God will tell you.

The second step to running with your dream, then, is to ask God for His guidance. Ask for what you want, or you will have to settle for what you get. Develop a personal relationship with God, and He will show you things to come.

> Ask me of things to come concerning my sons, and concerning the work of my hands command ye me. Isaiah 45:11

> Call unto me, and I will answer thee, and show thee great and mighty things, which thou knowest not. Jeremiah 33:3

> If ye abide in me, and my words abide in you, ye shall ask what ye will, and it shall be done unto you. John 15:7

In prayer one morning I said, "Lord, I want You to show me something that is going to happen to Your children, something new that I don't already know. I want to know something else concerning Your purpose for us." Then the Lord told me that He was going to open up British television to the Gospel. Now, I don't know when this is going to take place, but I do know that when it takes place, I will be there fulfilling my purpose in life.

After you have asked, expect to see God's guidance. A few years ago, Marte and I were preparing to leave for a pastors conference in Florida. I was talking to the Lord about this conference and He told me, "I'm sending you to Florida to encourage the pastors and to lift up their arms. Some of them have almost lost their vision, but you are going to rekindle this vision." I expected this to happen and this is exactly what happened. If God will do that for me, then He will do that for you.

The way you hear God's guidance is to build a close relationship with Him. If you will diligently seek God with all your heart, He will show you your purpose for living.

As you read God's Word continually and look for guidance in it, your spirit will grow. You'll become hungry for even more of His Word, the entrance of which gives light; it causes you to be able to see where you are going.[16]

> The spirit of man is the candle of the Lord,
> searching all the inward parts of the belly.
> Proverbs 20:27

But your spiritual candle will stay lit only as long as you stay filled with the oil of God's Spirit. This is done by spending more time in prayer. So let God light your candle and draw you out of the darkness into fulfillment. As you live in His presence, you will have energy that you didn't know you had, energy to be that person and to do those

[16]Psalm 119:130

things of which you've dreamed.

The next step is to decide what you want and then act upon it. The more you act, the larger your dream will grow. When you begin to act on your dream, it gets bigger and bigger.

No action is too small, but first you must decide what you want and then be willing to try. Before you can get out of your box you must want to get out. You must be willing to crawl before you walk, just as a baby crawls before he walks.

Do something every day toward fulfilling your dream. Gunder Birkeland pictured himself living his dream, and every day he rocked his box back and forth, trying to get out. In the end he was successful because he did not give up.

Start where you are with what you have, and God will give you more. During our first few years in the ministry, Marte and I installed peep holes in doors. These are little round holes which enable you to see outside before opening the door. The Lord gave us this little idea when we needed a financial blessing. Everyone we told about our idea thought it was funny, but their laughter ceased when I returned home that first day and emptied all the money out of my pockets. I had averaged twenty-two dollars an hour.

Let your dream motivate you. See yourself living your dream. When Gunder Birkeland was asked about his success he said, "Have a dream, and see yourself out of your box. You don't have to live in a box." It does not matter how small your dream is, because it will grow as you act on it.

Examine your dream in detail and know it inside and out. When I was growing up, I dreamed of being a designer and builder of houses, and I became the "world's greatest clubhouse builder." I used boards of odd shapes and sizes, remnants from construction jobs, or anything I could get my hands on and I built clubhouses—more than anyone else in town. I memorized the shape and size of every board in them; then I would take the clubhouse apart and build another style. I expected to become a builder, so I built clubhouses until I could build them without thinking about it.

Let your hopes stabilize your thinking. "Hope" means *to have confidence, to look with expectation to the fulfillment of something.* Expecting something good to happen stabilizes your thinking, emotions and life. But expecting something bad to happen sets your whole system out of balance and makes you nervous and jittery.

> Which hope we have as an anchor of the soul,
> both sure and stedfast, and which entereth into
> that within the veil.   Hebrews 6:19

At Word of Faith we have several video tape recorders. If we turn on these recorders without inserting a video tape or audio signal, the pictureless screen on the monitor becomes jittery and a lot of snowy static dances across it. If we run unrecorded video tape, then we get a steady snow pattern. But if we record the video, the tape is stabilized and a pattern appears that determines the picture. Thus without a video signal there is no pattern, but with one there is. So it is in your life.

There must be some "video" input; there must be some favorable expectations. By the way, in Latin *video* literally means "I see." Once you *see* your dreams and your goals in your spirit, you will accomplish them. You see, your dreams are *fond hopes or strong desires for something* and hopes are stabilized by "video" input.

Here's what happens. God drops a desire into your heart and He lets you see it in your spirit—*that desire in your spirit is the starting point of all achievement*. The Spirit of God is in that desire; energy and creativity are in it. Because it is a godly desire, it has a favorable expectation.

Thou hast given him his heart's desire.
                                                    Psalm 21:2

Act on your strong desires. Get excited! Desire acted on is power and the starting point of all achievement. Your action is what brings your desire into reality.

As a young man I designed houses and buildings. Even after Marte and I were saved, I continued to build California townhouses and other buildings. God put that desire in my heart, but then I became discouraged and stopped building.

Marte did not understand why I had stopped building if God had given me the desire. So she asked God and He told her, "I did call him to build houses. But now I am giving him a vision to build houses for My people and My glory."

Let your vision help you see the invisible. Your godly desire, like a vision, has the ability to see something not actually visible. It gives you the ability to see beyond what is and to bring about what should be. There are more things to see than the things you see in the natural. God can give you the ability to see things that are not yet visible. By looking beyond what is, you bring into reality what should be. God gives ordinary people visions so that they can do extraordinary things.

4

Run with Your Dream

With God's Word guiding you like a rudder and the wind of the Holy Ghost in your sails, you will move forward.

A man in our congregation at Word of Faith had a vision to buy a laundromat in a shopping center. Then he was given the opportunity to buy the shopping center. Now he owns several laundromats which have begun turning into shopping centers. This man's vision materialized when he acted on it. By operating in an environment of success you can do more things because success breeds success. Everything reproduces after its own kind. This man's vision helped him see the invisible. Once he started acting on that vision, God took him off the assembly line and made him an entrepreneur, a self-employed businessman, by God's power and for God's glory.

One of the ways God uses me is to fill believers with His Word and show them how to run with their dreams and visions. But there is a price to pay before you can see your dream come to pass.

> For a dream comes with much business and painful [diligent] effort.
>
> Ecclesiastes 5:3 (AMP)

God wants you to exercise diligent efforts. In the business world, strategic business decisions are based on facts only made available after exhaustive investigations. Decisions made without all the facts can be very costly. Successful executives know that success does not happen by accident. Success happens because certain principles are followed, and these principles are found in God's Word.

> But the man who looks intently into the perfect law that gives freedom, and continues to do this, not forgetting what he has heard, but doing it—he will be blessed in what he does.
>
> James 1:25 (NIV)

So the more you study God's Word the more you will learn about making good business decisions.

God wants you to look at the possibilities instead of problems. Then He will show you how to loose from the earth what you need to make your vision a reality. However, whether you see lack or abundance is up to you.

Several years ago, a Christian businessman dreamed of building a mobile home park in a particular suburb. Without looking at all the facts, he bought a piece of property at a good price. On going to see it he discovered that it did not have a city sewage line, so he decided to put in septic tanks. But when the soil was tested, the report showed that the soil was not of the right consistency to swallow sewage.

Now he understood why he had been able to buy the property at such a reasonable price. The previous developers had evidently already seen the soil report. However, instead of fretting he looked for a solution and God gave him the idea of installing his own solid waste disposal plant, without septic tanks.

His mobile home park, at that time, was one of the most beautiful parks in the area. The developers who sold him that property thought they had ripped him off because all they saw was failure, but he saw success.

A diligent man thinks bigger, not smaller. By seeing success and abundance he will end up with the wealth of the sinner.

The wealth of the sinner is laid up for the just.
                                    Proverbs 13:22

The thoughts of the diligent tend only to
plenteousness.   Proverbs 21:5

The hand of the diligent maketh rich.
                                    Proverbs 10:4

Jesus will give you the ability to see your dreams become reality. But it is important that you make Jesus Lord of:

- your life
- your family
- your business

Once He is, then all your actions will be blessed and He will show you how to run with your dream and acquire wealth so that He can establish His covenant in the earth.[17]

Being motivated by good will help you run with your dream. Sinners are motivated by greed and fear. Some believers are also motivated by fear until they become spiritual-minded.

For God hath not given us the spirit of fear;
but of power, and of love, and of a sound mind.
                                    II Timothy 1:7

Believers need to be motivated by faith so they can believe for the right things. But to have this faith they must not listen to the temptations of Satan.

Adam and Eve lost the vision of who they were because they yielded to Satan's temptation. The word "tempt" means *to entice someone to*

[17]Deuteronomy 8:18

commit an unwise or immoral act by promise of reward. Satan enticed Adam and Eve away from what was good. They lost their vision when they yielded to him and were no longer able to see things correctly; so they perished.

> Where there is no vision, the people perish.
> Proverbs 29:18

When you see things through the Word of God, the truth will set you free.

> Thy word is a lamp unto my feet, and a light unto my path. Psalm 119:105

> The light of the body is the eye: if therefore thine eye be single, thy whole body shall be full of light. Matthew 6:22

This is why Satan tries to blind your eyes to the truth in God's Word. He does not want you to have abundant life. He knows that what you see with your eyes is what you believe to be true.

Keep your vision sharp because the things you perceive are absorbed into your spirit and become a part of you. These things will influence your dream. The devil knows this, so he will try to stop you from seeing things correctly.

How you see things and what you believe determines your attitude. Having a positive attitude will help you react better to life. It will also cause life to react better to you. So pay close attention to your attitude. If two people walked into a room and one had a positive attitude and the other a negative one, who would be blessed?

You're right, the one with the positive attitude. Get this valuable information into your inner man and review it again and again until you fully understand it.

> The light of the body is the eye: if therefore thine eye be single, thy whole body shall be full of light.
> But if thine eye be evil, thy whole body shall be full of darkness. If therefore the light that is in thee be darkness, how great is that darkness!   Matthew 6:22-23

Your whole being is filled with light when you see things correctly, when you have the right attitude.

I remember the lean days of our early ministry. I prayed a lot for our needs, but I prayed also that God would help me to see things correctly, to see them like He saw them. I wanted to be a good provider for my family, but we were often broke between meetings. One day the Lord said to me, "Paul had a tent making job." I immediately knew that God wanted us to meet our financial needs by manual labor. So we began building cedar fences.

Can you imagine a preacher and his delicate little wife building fences? Marte unloaded the truck and I put up the fences. We worked hard building those fences, but we averaged $1,000 a week. At the end of two weeks, we paid our bills and headed back on the revival trail.

Now we could have said, "There's no way we can pay our bills." But we saw God as our source and believed there was a way. What we saw determined our attitude and controlled how we reacted to this situation.

When a lie is absorbed into your spirit you will not see things correctly until that lie is replaced with the truth. Several years ago, while I was ministering in another church, a woman with a broken leg came into the service. I wanted to preach her full of faith so she would get healed. So I walked up to the woman and said, "The Lord wants to heal you." But to my surprise she replied, "The devil didn't do this to me."

"The devil did this," I said.

"No," she answered, "God did this."

She actually believed that God had broken her leg, so she could not *see* her healing. She had forgotten that God sends only good to His children, and that health and healing are good.

> Every good gift and every perfect (free, large, full) gift is from above; it comes down from the Father of all [that gives] light, in [the shining of] Whom there can be no variation.
> James 1:17 (AMP)

And He will not tempt, test, or try a person with evil.

> Let no one say when he is tempted, I am tempted from God; for God is incapable of being tempted by [what is] evil **and He Himself tempts no one.**   James 1:13 (AMP)

Satan, on the other hand, tries to move you away from good; he tries to move you from happiness with unhappiness. He tries to move you away from joy with sorrow. He will say, "Oh, have a little pity party. Everything is bad. It is a blue day. It's raining outside." Perhaps it is raining outside, but above those clouds the sun is shining. The sun is always shining. It never stops shining. You will see what you want to see: the rain or the sunshine, the problems or the solutions, sickness or health.

What you see on the inside determines what you see on the outside. "If thine eye be evil, thy whole body shall be full of darkness."[18] Your viewpoint makes all the difference. If your understanding is darkened, what you see is darkness. To keep the devil from defeating you, you must get it right on the inside.

One way to get it right on the inside is to look through eyes of faith. See your dream by faith in your spirit. Become pregnant with your dream and let it grow and mature inside your spirit. Nurture it with faith. Keep hearing the Word of God because faith comes from hearing the Word.[19]

I want you to see yourself as a big sailing ship. Your dream is your sail. It represents your purpose in life and determines the direction your ship goes. Without a dream you are like a boat without a sail.

[18]Matthew 6:23   [19]Romans 10:17

Harbors are full of boats going nowhere because their sails are not hoisted. It does not matter whether you have many little sails or one big sail; until your sail is set into the wind of the Holy Ghost your dream will not go anywhere.

Your dream, like the sail, is what moves you forward. So let your dream set the sails of your boat. Then with God's Word guiding you like a rudder and the wind of the Holy Ghost in your sails, you will move forward.

The size of your boat determines the size and number of sails you need. A little boat requires a little sail and does little things. A big boat uses many sails, both large and small, and does bigger things. Sailors learned a long time ago that it is better to have a whole bunch of little sails headed in the right direction than to have just one big one. Then if one needs repair, there are other sails to keep the ship moving. But don't add a second sail until you have learned to use the first.

Several years ago, I became complacent and disinterested about several facets of my dream and vision for Word of Faith. I had stopped acting on my dream, because I was no longer motivated by it. Then one day I realized what had happened. The devil had knocked the wind out of my sails.

To a certain extent I had lost my vision. I had not stopped working for the Lord, but I did not have the intense energy and enthusiasm I normally had. "Enthusiasm" comes from the Greek word *enthousiazien* which means *to be inspired by God*. I had lost my inspiration and my first love.

As I meditated on this, I realized I had stopped visualizing my dream so my sail had been pulled down. I also realized that there are two ways you can strengthen your dream and keep it in front of you:

- Meditate on it
- Plan it step by step

I needed to associate myself with my vision again, so I surrounded myself with pictures, graphs and other things having to do with my dream. Then as I meditated, the wind of the Holy Spirit began to blow and I set sail again.

Through this I learned that your dream is your future, and what you see in your future gives your dream power. You are either giving power to the future or the past with its problems, discouragements, lack of opportunities and bitterness.

So choose to see through the eyes of faith. Elisha's servant cried out in fear when he saw the enemy surrounding the city of Dothan.[20] His servant saw the enemy, but Elisha, looking at the situation through eyes of faith, saw the promises of God. This is why he could respond, "Fear not: for they that be with us are more than they that be with them."[21] He then asked God to open his servant's eyes, so that he too could see the victory.

[20] II Kings 6:15 [21] II Kings 6:16

I want God to open your eyes so you can see more:

- solutions than problems
- health than sickness
- success than failure
- opportunities than lack

Through the eyes of faith, we do see things. Not natural things, but things that are not seen—spiritual things.

> While we look not at the things which are seen, but at the things which are not seen: for the things which are seen are temporal; but the things which are not seen are eternal.
>
> II Corinthians 4:18

Choose to see through the dream that God has given you. Acts 2 reveals that in the last days people will have dreams and visions and be able to see things. God Himself dreams and He put dreaming inside you so that you could chart your course in life.

> And it shall come to pass in the last days, saith God, I will pour out of my Spirit upon all flesh: and....your young men shall see visions, and your old men shall dream dreams.
>
> Acts 2:17

Once you see things through faith's eyes, you will be able to chart your course by God's dream in your heart. Then you will see an abundance of good things come into your life.

God wants you to hear the sound of abundance, even though others can only see lack.

Elijah heard the sound of an abundance of rain before it was visible.[22] There had been a drought in Israel for three and a half years, and Elijah got down on his knees and began to pray for rain. After awhile, he said to his servant, "I hear the abundance of rain. Go and look."

The servant went up to Mount Carmel and came back saying, "Elijah, I don't see anything."

"You didn't see anything? I hear the sound of abundance. Can't you hear it? Are you sure you don't hear it?" Elijah said.

Elijah got back on his knees. The Scriptures say he prayed seven times. At first, I didn't understand that. Now I believe that he was saying, "Lord, I hear abundance." Every time he got back up, he would hear abundance again.

Abundance is all that I hear. I can't help it any longer. I haven't heard lack for a long time; I don't even know what it sounds like, and I don't want to know because I am hearing abundance.

Seven times Elijah got down on his knees. And seven times he got up and said to his servant, "Get back up there to that mountaintop. Don't you dare come back and tell me you see nothing. Get back up there."

Eventually, the servant saw a small cloud the size of a man's hand. When he reported the cloud to Elijah, Elijah took off running because he knew that great rains were on their way. He had seen abundance.

[22]I Kings 18:41, 44-45

This reminds me of a woman who listened to my radio program and heard me say that God would heal anyone who would get some tapes and listen to healing scriptures from the Bible. The doctors had sent her home to die. She had a draining, cancerous tumor in her breast, and the doctors had said there was nothing they could do for her since the cancer had spread throughout her body.

She bought my tapes on healing and began to listen to them. But after a week, she got mad and called me on the telephone, saying, "They didn't work. I didn't get healed."

At first I thought, "Oh no. I've got a problem!" Suddenly righteous indignation rose up inside me. I no longer saw sickness in that woman. I saw health in her, so I said, "How dare you tell me God is a liar! How dare you tell me that God's Word doesn't work! You turn those tapes on, and don't call me back until you are out of that bed, walking, and healed by the power of God."

Three weeks later I got another telephone call from her, but this time she was shouting, "Hallelujah! Hallelujah! Hallelujah!

"Brother Tilton," she said, "I listened to those tapes over and over, then I really began to *hear* them. When I heard that I was healed by the stripes of Jesus, the power of God went through my body and closed those festering cancerous holes. I got out of bed immediately, and I have been dancing and praising God ever since. I'm healed by the power of God!" This woman stopped hearing sickness and started hearing healing and health.

You, too, can stop hearing sickness, lack, discouragement and sorrow. You can hear the sound of God's abundance, joy, love and blessings on you, your household and your business.

Run with your dream. If you don't have one, get on your knees and pray until God shows you what He created you for. When your dream comes, it will be just a little spark. But it only takes a little spark to light a huge fire.

Listen to these words the Lord spoke to me one morning while I was praying, and think on them.

> If you will learn to walk by the things not seen, you can have the things you desire that are seen.

Seeing things through faith's eyes will allow you to run and not be weary.

> But they that wait upon the Lord shall renew their strength; they shall mount up with wings as eagles; they shall run, and not be weary; and they shall walk, and not faint.
>
> Isaiah 40:31

Then you will be able to fly above your problems, instead of having to live in the middle of them.

As long as Peter looked to Jesus he walked above the circumstances. But when he began to see the waves and smell, hear, and feel the wet winds, he began to sink.[23] As long as Peter kept his vision, he did fine. He was either being moved by Jesus, by what he saw in his spirit, or he was moved by what he saw in the natural. You are either being drawn to the solution or to the problem and failure. You have the power of choice: good or evil, blessing or cursing.

> I call heaven and earth to record this day against you, that I have set before you life and death, blessing and cursing: therefore choose life, that both thou and thy seed may live.
> Deuteronomy 30:19

Looking at your problems will drain your strength, but looking at the Word of God will revitalize you. Look to Jesus! See your dream through the eyes of God; see your dream through the eyes of faith.

When your course in life is charted by God's dream in your heart, whatever you do will prosper.[24] In the process of building Word of Faith Family Church, we have attended many city council meetings and have been told "No," dozens of times. But all we could hear was "Yes." And we always got what we needed for the Lord's work.

> Seest thou a man diligent in his business? he shall stand before kings; he shall not stand before mean [obscure] men.
> Proverbs 22:29

> The thoughts of the diligent tend only to plenteousness.
> Proverbs 21:5

[23]Matthew 14:28-30 [24]Psalm 1:3

The hand of the diligent maketh rich.

Proverbs 10:4

A good man out of the good treasure of his
heart bringeth forth good things.

Matthew 12:35

By the authority of Jesus Christ, by the greatest
vision a person can ever have—and that is seeing Christ in you, the hope, the image of God—I
release healing, health, and miracles into your life
this very moment. I prophesy miracles to you.
Come on! Reach out and take it. Turn your faith
loose. Chart your course. Get out of the box.
Stand up and walk—in the name of Jesus Christ.

A Word from the Lord for You

Do not look back, but look forward and
you will see the right direction. I gave Lot
a way of escape, and you will see your way
of escape if you look forward. Lot's wife
looked back and she failed, but Lot looked
forward and escaped from the destruction
behind him.

5

Chart Your Course

The position of your rudder and set of your sail, not the wind's force, causes your boat to move in the right direction.

You have the power of choice. As a free moral agent you can choose your direction in life. God has given you the power to choose good over evil and blessing over cursing.

> I call heaven and earth to record this day against you, that I have set before you life and death, blessing and cursing: therefore choose life, that both thou and thy seed may live:
> Deuteronomy 30:19

However, you need to seek direction from God. By basing your decisions on God's Word, you are assured that you are not going against His will. God wants to help you choose your direction in life, and He does this by charging your spirit with creative ability. Then He lets you make decisions for yourself and act on the inspirations He places in your spirit.[25]

I know a young man who has a God-given talent for writing songs that glorify and magnify God. But even though he enjoys God's inspiration, he alone must decide the direction to go with his talent.

Many people choose their direction by the things they see. Some of us like to say that we are not moved by what we see. But the truth is we *are* moved by what we see. Either we see things in the natural with the limitations of natural laws or in the spiritual with no limitations. We then base our judgments and actions on what we see—regardless of whether it is natural or spiritual.

Spiritual sight comes from attending to God's Word and brings us into unlimited abundant life. Once you have this spiritual sight, you will not need to depend on your natural senses alone for direction in life.

Like a road map, God's Word, through your spiritual sight, guides and directs your life. His Word helps you stay on the right road and your

[25]Job 32:8

obedience to the guidelines found in it guarantees you a safe trip. But disobedience can cause you to run off the edge of the road.

Some who do not know God seek this direction through the occult:

- consulting fortune tellers
- reading their horoscope

A few believers are even fooled into using the things of the occult. Perhaps this is because they have never been told that these things are counterfeits of the real. Satan never does anything original, and is a counterfeiter and perverter of the truth. Ouija boards, palm reading, crystal balls, tarot cards, horoscopes, and séances are counterfeits for the gifts of the Holy Spirit.

There is *only one* person who can give you a real purpose for living, and His name is Jesus Christ.[26] But a large percentage of the world does not know Him as the true God, so they do not ask Him for direction. Instead, they search for a sign from their gods, hoping these will give them a purpose and a direction in life.

Over the years I have watched people constantly follow signs, trying to find a direction for their lives. "If the interest rates are right tomorrow...if the weather is right..." they say. They program their minds daily by reading the newspaper or by listening to news reports. "The economy looks bad and gasoline prices are going up, so I'd better not do anything," they murmur.

[26]Jeremiah 33:3

Unfortunately, they do not realize that God is able to fill up their gas tank with gasoline whatever the price.

I have even noticed some Christians looking continuously for the right sign. "If the right door opens up, then I'll know it's the will of God," or "Well, this door opened up so it must be the will of God." But these are natural signs, and their guidance can be false. If you follow them you may never reach your destination.

Then there are some who try to put a fleece for direction before the Lord, as Gideon did. However, Gideon placed the fleece before the Lord because he was not spiritual enough to make God his covenant partner.[27] At that time Israel was dead spiritually, so God had to speak to the people through their natural senses. But you and I are alive spiritually, and God speaks to us through His Word and His Holy Spirit.

Let signs follow you, instead of your following signs. Signs will not help you find God's perfect will for your life. Only by studying His Word and acting on it will you find God's perfect will.

As a child of God you are a joint-heir with Jesus. He lives in you and wants to work through you;[28] therefore, you do not need to follow signs like the world does.

> The Spirit itself beareth witness with our spirit, that we are the children of God:

[27]Judges 6:13 [28]Galatians 2:20

> And if children, then heirs; heirs of God,
> and joint-heirs with Christ; if so be that we suf-
> fer with him, that we may be also glorified
> together.   Romans 8:16-17

However, when you act on God's Word, signs will follow you.

> And THESE SIGNS SHALL FOLLOW THEM
> THAT BELIEVE; In my name shall they cast
> out devils; they shall speak with new tongues.
>   Mark 16:17

When you tell others about healing and prosperity, then healing and prosperity will follow you. But telling others about sickness and lack will cause sickness and lack to follow you. Signs follow what you preach, and words reproduce themselves the way you believe them. Perhaps the things taking place in your life today are your past words following you.

You determine your destiny. "Determine" means *to decide, to establish, to cause or make*. God has given you power to determine your direction in life. The choice is yours, but you must decide what you want. God put that dream in your heart, and He has also given you the desire to see your dream come into being.

It is the position of the rudder (God's Word) and set of the sail (your dream), not the wind's force, that moves the boat in the right direction. You can either make things happen or let things happen. God has given you the authority to make things happen in agreement with His Word.

> I will give you the keys of the kingdom of
> heaven; whatever you bind on earth will be
> bound in heaven, and whatever you loose on
> earth will be loosed in heaven."
>
> Matthew 16:19 (NIV)

Recently, the Lord spoke these words to me: "I cannot loose from Heaven what you don't loose on earth." As part of the Body of Christ you have the authority to loose Heaven's resources and God's will into the earth. By using the keys of the kingdom you will overcome all of Satan's hindrances.

Let me give you an example. I have an electronic garage door opener. When I pull up in front of my house and push the little button, up goes the garage door. I pull my car into the garage. Why? Because I have authority to go in there. Everything in it belongs to me. I can park my car, put the door down, walk into my house, take off my shoes, plop down on the couch, and enjoy what belongs to me. This garage door opener makes everything in my garage accessible to me. It is the key and I use it.

That's the way it is with the kingdom of God, but the keys to the kingdom are voice activated; God has given you the authority to speak His will.

> Death and life are in the power of the tongue:
> and they that love it shall eat the fruit thereof.
>
> Proverbs 18:21

We can eat the fruit of Heaven now—the fruit of eternal life, the fruit of the Spirit (love, joy, peace, longsuffering, gentleness, goodness, faith, meekness, temperance). This fruit is just the earnest or down payment of a whole lot more to come. Jesus said, "Ask, and it shall be given you...for every one that asketh receiveth."[29] If you don't ask, you will have to settle for what you get.

> You shall also decide and decree a thing and it shall be established for you, and the light [of God's favor] shall shine upon your ways.
> Job 22:28 (AMP)

You can predict your future. Some people may disagree with this statement, but it is scriptural. The word "predict" means *to foretell what will happen, or to tell something in advance*. It takes faith to predict your future. You predict your future and determine your destiny by your vision, by what you see in your heart.

> Where there is no vision, the people perish.
> Proverbs 29:18

Your vision is your future. A "vision" is *the ability to see something that is not visible in the natural*. Picture your future as a wall standing a great distance ahead of you. But as you walk toward that wall the distance becomes less and the wall gets closer. Now suppose that wall were invisible, but you knew it was there. That is a vision. It is something not seen in the natural.

When Marte and I started out in the ministry we had a vision in our spirit, but that vision was still a great distance ahead of us. Nevertheless, we walked toward our vision until we were close

[29]Matthew 7:7-8

enough to touch it and see it become reality. We could have stayed away from the vision, or walked in a different direction, and it would have remained a vision, but it would not have become real to us. But instead we charted our course by the vision in our hearts and it became reality.

A number of years ago, God gave a young couple a vision of teaching worship and praise in the churches across America. This couple followed their vision as God directed them, one step at a time. But even though they were faithful, the churches whose doors were opened to them had only 25 to 100 members.

One day, they asked the Lord to show them how to bring their vision to pass quicker. About this time I met them and told them I felt they could be a great blessing to the Body of Christ by leading worship and praise for our television satellite services. In this way, they would be fulfilling their vision and releasing to the Body of Christ the anointing God had placed on them.

This couple had acted on their vision right from the beginning, although at times it did not seem like much. But they believed that their faithfulness would bring their vision into full realization.

A lot of people are never able to realize their full potential in life, because they cannot see the unseen by faith. They fail to realize that the future is predicted through the unseen.

> Through faith we understand that the worlds
> were framed by the word of God, so that things
> which are seen were not made of things which
> do appear.   Hebrews 11:3

> While we look not at the things which are seen,
> but at the things which are not seen.
>   II Corinthians 4:18

Walking according to the leading of God's Spirit
is a walk of faith. God wants to give you the things
you desire, but you must learn to walk by things
that are not seen.[30]

Faith will bring your vision into reality because
it is like a preprogrammed seed. Jesus said a seed
has the capability of knowing its future, and the
ability within itself to predict that future. He told
the disciples that if they had faith the size of a
mustard seed whatever they said would come to
pass.

> And the Lord said, If ye had faith as a grain
> of mustard seed, ye might say unto this
> sycamine tree, Be thou plucked up by the root,
> and be thou planted in the sea; and it should
> obey you.   Luke 17:6

God programmed His Word in seed form to go
wherever He willed and to never return void or
without fruit. Your faith comes from hearing the
Word. That's why it is important to hide His Word
in your heart and to allow it to produce fruit.

Not long ago, while I was out in my garden,
I noticed some weeds that had not been there a
few days earlier.

[30]Hebrews 11:3

"Where did these weeds come from?" I asked the gardener.

"When the soil gets hot, the seeds in it start popping open and the weeds start coming up," he replied.

At that moment, the Lord gave me insight into spiritual seeds and spiritual growth. Seeds— whether good or bad, flowers or weeds—grow when the soil is hot. That's why it is important for you to be enthusiastic and excited about God. When you are, the seeds—the Word of God inside you—will start popping open, growing and bringing forth much fruit. And one of the most important fruits of the Word is faith.

The level of your faith determines what you see and how far you see. When Peter saw Jesus walking on the water his faith soared, until he could see himself walking to Jesus on the water.[31]

When I pray for the sick, I believe they are healed by the stripes of Jesus.[32] In my spirit, I see them healed, and I predict their healing by a word of faith.

It is important to confess the Word of God. By confessing the Word you are foretelling what you believe is going to happen before it ever happens. Many people let the past influence them, and instead of foretelling what the Word of God says is going to happen, they only repeat what has already happened, what they already have.

[31]Matthew 14:29   [32]Isaiah 53:5

This is what happens when God's Word is not mature in your spirit. Confessing the Word of God plants it in your spirit so it can mature and bring forth fruit.

God's Word, like a seed, is preprogrammed to bear fruit. Just like seed, it has to be sown in good soil, watered and tended. Some Christians carry God's Word (the *logos*) around with them, but never let it become *rhema* (alive) in their spirit.

Natural seeds reproduce themselves through a process called germination. The word "germinate" means *to grow, to mature, or to sprout*. The soil must contain the right ingredients for nourishment for a seed to germinate.

(1) A germinating seed must have adequate amounts of *oxygen* to produce the energy needed for growth. The taking in of oxygen and the giving off of carbon dioxide causes a seed to burn food which then produces the energy needed for growth.

God's Word needs energy for growth. And the Holy Spirit burning inside you produces this energy.[33] However, the cares of this world can choke out the Word of God in you, and cause it to die.

(2) A germinating seed must have *light* to make food. In the parable of the sower some people heard the Word, but the devil was able to destroy their seed because they did not understand what they heard.[34]

[33]Psalm 39:3 [34]Matthew 13:19

"Understand" means *to have light on the subject, or to be enlightened*. When you understand God's Word it then becomes food for growth in your spirit.

(3) A germinating seed needs large amounts of *moisture* or water. Moisture causes certain chemical changes to occur in a seed which enable it to grow into a plant.

If your spirit is not watered by God's Spirit, you will become dry and indifferent to the things of God and His Word will no longer be or become *rhema* to your spirit.

(4) A germinating seed needs *heat*. Seeds remain dormant (inactive) as long as the temperature outside is cold.

God's Word remains dormant in you as long as you are cold and indifferent to the things of God. The Word of God cannot grow and produce fruit in your life without the fire of the Holy Spirit.

God's Word contains a harvest of good things for you. It is full of seeds preprogrammed to bring victory, health, and success, but first you must accept them as truth. What you accept in your spirit as truth determines what you believe. And what you believe controls your actions, and regulates your level of success in life.

When truth becomes *rhema* (the living Word) in your spirit, you will see the answer to your need. When this *rhema* is infused into your need and then spoken, it becomes *phemi* (the spoken

Word), the prophesied will of God for you. What you believe in your heart and speak with words of faith regulates the amount of God's grace and favor released from Heaven into the earth and into your life.

Prophetically speak the Word of God to your life, your home, your loved ones, your business. Personalize the Word of God and speak the will of God. You can prophesy.

But you cannot prophesy beyond your level of faith. Going beyond your faith or beyond what the Scriptures promise gets you into presumption and foolishness. Romans 12:6 says you prophesy according to what you have faith for. You can only decree what you can see through the eye of faith.

> For I say, through the grace given unto me, to every man that is among you, not to think of himself more highly than he ought to think; but to think soberly, according as God hath dealt to every man the measure of faith.
>
> Romans 12:3
>
> Having then gifts differing according to the grace that is given to us, whether prophecy, let us prophesy according to the proportion of faith. Romans 12:6

A few years ago, I felt Satan coming against this ministry. Immediately, the Spirit of God rose up in me and said, "Prophesy life! Prophesy according to your proportion of faith."

I began to prophesy, "TV program, get back in line. I'm speaking to you and I command you to line up with the rest of this ministry. Bible

school, I speak life into you. Darkness, depart in
Jesus' name. Light, come back in Jesus' name.

"Staff, come together in Jesus' name. Staff,
walk in harmony; walk in love; walk in faith. I
prophesy that God is sending us workers who are
qualified, born again, Spirit-filled; workers who
are walking in the Word, in love and in
forgiveness. I prophesy that our staff will come
in from every direction—north, south, east, and
west." I prophesied our future.

You can prophesy yours too. You are God's
child; you are feeding on His Word and drinking
of His Spirit. Sooner or later you will be conformed to His image; you will become Christlike.
The Spirit of God told me that whatever is in your
heart is going to come out of your mouth. It is
important to guard your heart, because what
comes out of your heart gives substance to your
dreams and visions.

> For out of the abundance of the heart the mouth
> speaketh.   Matthew 12:34

> Keep your heart with all vigilance and above all
> that you guard, for out of it flow the springs
> of life [the stuff dreams are made of].
>   Proverbs 4:23 (AMP)

That's how you prophesy: you speak forth the
Word of God that is in your heart and apply it
to your future. "Prophecy" is *a prediction of
something you believe is going to happen before
it ever happens, or a declaration of divine will*.
Everyone wants results in their lives, but results

come by the Word of God becoming *rhema* (alive) in you. Only then will you prosper spiritually, physically, and financially.

> Beloved, I wish above all things that thou mayest prosper and be in health, even as thy soul prospereth.   III John 2

But prophecy has some prerequisites. A "prerequisite" is *something that is required as a prior condition to something else*. When I attended college I wanted to major in architecture, but I had to take math first. Math was a prerequisite; it was required beforehand. Paul in the book of Romans gives us God's prerequisites for those who would prophesy.

> I beseech you therefore, brethren, by the mercies of God, that ye present your bodies a living sacrifice, holy, acceptable unto God, which is your reasonable service.
>
> And be not conformed to this world: but be ye transformed by the renewing of your mind, that ye may prove what is that good, and acceptable, and perfect, will of God.
>   Romans 12:1-2

Prerequisite #1: Your body is to be presented to God as a living sacrifice. In other words, reckon your natural senses dead, and alive only when they agree with the Word of God. No longer do you need to be conformed to this world, because you are transformed.

The Greek word for transformed used here is *metamorphoo*. It is from this word that we get the word metamorphosis. A caterpillar goes through a metamorphosis (transformation) before it becomes a butterfly. You, too, will go through a metamorphosis as you present your thoughts and life to God. He will transform you into His image and make you think His thoughts.

Prerequisite #2: The renewing of your mind will transform you into the image and likeness of Christ[35] so that you can "prove what is that good, and acceptable, and perfect, will of God." This will allow you to prophesy the truth, speak the truth and know the truth.

As you become more Christlike, the *logos* will become *rhema* to you. As you line up your situation with the Word of God and take the *rhema* and turn it into *phemi*, you will prophesy your dream.

> Thou shalt also decree a thing, and it shall be established unto thee: and the light shall shine upon thy ways.   Job 22:28

In 1976, the auditorium of the Word of Faith Family Church here in Dallas was nothing but a dream. Nevertheless, God allowed me to prophesy the future of the church:

> I prophesy to you in the name of the Lord Jesus Christ that this church will rise up from this situation and go forth. You will see people fly here from all over the world, trying to figure out how we did it. They will find the Word of God operating in the hearts and lives of God's people because they have been fired up to work.

[35]Romans 8:29

At that time we were holding services in an old warehouse, and our church attendance was about 100. We kept putting out more and more chairs as that small congregation grew. Then we had blueprints drawn for the new church and construction got under way. It took about a year to get past the steel framework stage.

It seemed that every devil in hell was coming against us. After the framework was up, we ran out of money and it seemed that we couldn't get anything else done. Soon people started laughing at us and said that there was a crack in the foundation and the whole building would collapse. Others said the framework would rust and we would have to start over.

But I would stand right in the middle of the auditorium and speak to those metal rafters. I would prophesy, "Bones! Building! Girders! Come together and be clothed! Building, be clothed with tilt-up concrete walls. Be clothed with a nice roof. I command you to have a ceiling. I command you to have carpet on the floor. I command you to have fountains and trees in the lobby. I command you to have beautiful colors. I command you to have a concrete parking lot, not asphalt, nor a muddy, gravel lot."

I prophesied it for days. In the natural, it didn't look as if anything was happening. But in the supernatural, the Spirit of God was moving. The powers of darkness were being shaken. They were being pulled down. The blessings of God and the abundance of rain were beginning to come in so that we could start building again. And we built and built until the first phase of the construction was completed.

Then we built the second phase, and the third, and the fourth, and so on, until today our property—facilities and land—is valued at over $30 million, and it is all paid for. The principles in this book will work if you will work them!

Through the years, we have had many giants coming against us, but God continued giving me big dreams. And I prophesied them as the written Word became *rhema* (the living Word) to me.

Another person with big dreams was Michelangelo, a leading sculptor during the Renaissance. One day as he walked down the cobblestone streets of his city, a block of stone caught his attention and he inquired about it.

The stone seller, knowing Michelangelo's reputation, tried to talk him into looking at a better block of granite.

But in a clear voice Michelangelo said, "That block of stone is very important to me. I see something in it."

"What do you see?" the stone seller asked.

"I see an angel in that stone," Michelangelo replied, "and I must free him."

If you are having big dreams but not seeing them come into reality, don't lose patience. Don't give up! Prophesy to those dreams according to your level of faith, and chart your course in life by God's dreams in your heart. Continue to plant God's Word in your heart and let it become *rhema* to you. Eventually, your dream will become a reality if you keep walking toward it. Eventually, you will see your dream and free (loose) it.

6

Decree Your Destiny

Jesus Christ is behind your decree, and His authority is more powerful than any authority on the earth.

God thinks big thoughts and dreams big dreams, and He likes being around people who try to be like Him—people who dream big dreams. I'm a dreamer. Our church is loaded with dreamers. I believe that's because dreamers attract dreamers. Everyone in the church is constantly getting inspired ideas. I think it's great. I love it!

You can be a dreamer, too! Inspired ideas come when your thoughts are in agreement with God's will. One definition of "inspired" is *to be guided or controlled by divine influence*. By spending time in God's Word, you become sensitive to His voice and able to communicate with Him. He then infuses your spirit with creative ideas which, when you act on them, succeed.

> Roll your works upon the Lord—commit and trust them wholly to Him; [He will cause your thoughts to become agreeable to His will, and] so shall your plans be established and succeed.
>
> Proverbs 16:3 (AMP)

When I was building houses, I would sometimes drive my truck down the street and "windshield the job"—check on the job's progress without stopping. I especially enjoyed driving past a house that had been finished and its owners had already moved in and the children were playing in the yard. It felt good to see something I had created making others happy. It felt good to see my dream fulfilled.

But a dream must be watered, nourished, and kept away from the enemy. One of the major ways you protect a dream is by being careful of what you see. We are moved by what we see. That's why it is important that we see the eternal things of God, that we fight the good fight of faith and lay hold of new creation truths and realities.

We can say we have a vision when we are able to see things that cannot be seen in the natural, for a vision is the ability to look beyond what is and to bring about what should be.

Since we are moved by what we see, it is important that we avoid the dream stealers, whatever their credentials or whoever they might be.

Where there is no vision, the people perish.
Proverbs 29:18

The next step is to be faithful with what God gives you. Sometimes that may be only a small idea, but that idea will grow. So be faithful with the little things God gives, and then He will give bigger ideas.

When Marte and I first started out in the ministry, sometimes it was a month between meetings and then it might only be a one-night engagement. So we needed money to live on. One day Marte had an inspired idea.

"Bob," she said, "I think we should make Christian greeting cards. I'll find some appropriate scriptures, if you will draw little pictures to go with them. Then we can get them printed and sell them in the bookstores of the towns we go through."

I thought that was a great idea, and soon we had the cards printed. Everyone liked our cards, and usually would buy six packages, one of each of six designs. That was about $1.50 profit, but it might have cost us $4 or $5 in gas just to find the bookstore. So we committed the problem to the Lord.

A few days later I had another inspired idea while we were driving down the freeway from Dallas to Houston. I saw a cedar shadowbox with those cards stacked in it.

"Marte, we've been going into bookstores trying to sell one package. We should sell them seventy," I said. Then I explained to her about the shadowbox which would measure about one and one-half feet by two feet and hold seventy greeting card packages.

So we started making these shadowboxes from cedar pickets which we bought from a fence company and cardboard which we found in dumpsters behind mattress stores. I cut the cedar pickets to size, nailed the racks together with finishing nails, and placed the cardboard on the back of the rack with a stapler. Then Marte filled each rack with seventy packages of greeting cards.

We spoke the Word and favor of God over each rack. Then we agreed in prayer that when we walked into a store everyone would want to buy our cards. Soon the inside of our little travel trailer was solid greeting cards and racks.

When I went into a bookstore to show the cards, I always set up our display rack next to the cash register, and whoever was checking out would always want to buy cards even before we had sold them to the store. And the store manager would immediately want to buy the cards.

At night, we would pull into an inexpensive trailer park and look for an electric plug so that we could make some more racks. I would go to the lumberyard and get the pickets to make more racks while Marte folded the cards. She became the world's greatest card folder. Having them folded at the printers cost an extra one-fourth of a cent per card, and that added up. She could do it better than a folding machine, anyway. She was just like a robot, folding cards by the thousands and counting them into bundles of ten, while I cut pickets and nailed boxes together.

About 90 percent of the bookstores bought the racks with cards, and we sold an average of five to seven racks per day. Our profits from the greeting card racks averaged from $100 to $150 dollars a day. I know this may seem funny and maybe even foolish, but we were faithfully using the idea God had given us to put money in our pockets so that we could pursue our dream and continue traveling for Jesus.

And one inspired idea always leads to another. Our next idea was to wrap the cards in plastic so that they would look professional. We bought a roll of shrink film plastic, the kind big companies use. We didn't know you had to have a $2,500 machine to wrap the bundle and put it into a little oven at the exact heat to shrink the plastic to a nice, neat, pretty package. Nor did we know we needed a special machine to cut the plastic all around and to seal it airtight. So we bought a soldering iron for $2.50 and used it as a cutter. Then we used Marte's hair dryer for the oven. But we managed to heat-shrink our card packages.

Everyone loved them! People from all over began ordering cards. Within four months we were selling greeting cards in seven states. I am sure that if we had stayed with it we could have become as big as some of the other Christian greeting card companies.

When God gives you an inspired idea, take it. If He gives you several new ideas, develop them all. Do what you can. Our greeting card project started with one tiny idea which came into being when we released our desire to have enough money to live on.

A desire is the tiny starting point of all achievement. Desire acted upon is power. When you begin to release your desires and act upon them, things begin to happen. Things begin to move, and events begin working to bring those things to pass.

The fulfillment of one of our desires was the building of the Word of Faith Family Church auditorium. After a year of frustrations and delays, we were going to have our dedication service with no carpet, no lights, no ceiling tile in the bathrooms, no doors on the building, and with a parking lot full of junk.

The city had granted us a one-day permit and the members and workmen had worked all night for several nights trying to get the building halfway presentable. In the natural, it didn't look as though we had a building, but when we came for our dedication service, we saw the building as finished.

At 4:30 in the morning on the day of the dedication service, the Spirit of the Lord awakened me with three words—decide, decree, declare. Like little feathers they drifted into my spirit, each one on top of the other.

This is what the Lord said:

You have faithfully practiced the principles and the laws of My Word. Many times you did things even though you did not understand the reason, but they got results. You have practiced the laws and principles in My Word, and I am going to tell you three things that will make it easier for you. And I want you to tell them to others—**Decide, Decree, Declare.**

Number one: You made a decision. You determined what you were going to do.

Number two: You have been decreeing it. You have been confessing it. You have been saying it.

Number three: You have been declaring it.

The truth in those words continues to grow in me like a gigantic tree. However, no matter how much knowledge and inspiration I receive from them, it still boils down to three words—decide, decree, declare.

You shall also decide and decree a thing and
it shall be established for you, and the light [of
God's favor] shall shine upon your ways.
Job 22:28 (AMP)

First decide what you want. Your decision
determines your direction and destiny. You drive
a stake in the ground and declare, "This is it."
Your dream is conceived in your spirit at the time
you believe it can come to pass.

Then decree that you have the dream. Once
your dream is birthed in prayer and conceived
in your spirit, decree it. This establishes it and
orders it done.

Earthly decrees are backed by natural laws,
but a believer's decree is backed by God's spiritual
laws. When you make your decree in Jesus'
name, you have Christ's authority and power
behind you. And this authority is far more
powerful than any earthly authority.

Part of decreeing your dream is watering and
nourishing it by the reading of God's Word.
Country folks have wonderful gardens with all
kinds of vegetables in them. If they faithfully
water the gardens, they will reap abundant
healthy produce. However, if they fail to keep
their garden watered, the vegetables will shrivel
up and die. Reading and meditating on God's
Word will keep the fruit of your dream from
withering and dying.

Another part of decreeing is protecting your dream from life's adversities. I have seen the wonderful dreams of others destroyed by the storms of life and mountains of adversity.

Satan wants you to believe that your mountain of adversity can't be moved. But your mountain will be removed when you start looking at the things not seen, instead of things seen.

> While we look not at the things which are seen,
> but at the things which are not seen.
> II Corinthians 4:18

Stop looking at your mountain, and start looking at its successful removal. How you see things determines how you act or react to the opportunities around you. Success is seeing your dream come to pass with all obstacles moved out of the way.

Above all else, you must believe that the mountain can be moved. Remember the familiar scripture:

> And Jesus answering saith unto them, Have faith in God.
> For verily I say unto you, That whosoever shall say unto this mountain, Be thou removed, and be thou cast into the sea; and shall not doubt in his heart, but shall believe that those things which he saith shall come to pass; he shall have whatsoever he saith.
> Therefore I say unto you, What things soever ye desire, when ye pray, believe that ye receive them, and ye shall have them.
> Mark 11:22-24

This passage was one of the first scriptural revelations that Marte and I had in the beginning of our ministry. In the King James Version Mark 11:22 reads, "Have faith *in* God," but the literal Greek in this passage reads, "Have the faith *of* God." Romans 12:3 tells us that God has given each of us a measure of faith. Once you have the faith of God, you can move all adversities and mountains out of your way.

Many times Marte and I have been surrounded by mountains of adversity. One time the only transportation we had was a broken-down pickup truck. That ugly truck had four slick tires, both mufflers broken off, an outdated inspection sticker, and a paper license plate.

We were between meetings; it was cold, rainy and sleeting, and our little travel trailer was parked in a rundown trailer park. Then one night, as we pulled into the park, one of those slick tires went flat. We didn't ever have a spare. Nor did we have the money to get it fixed, so I totally ignored it.

Now if you had asked us, we would have told you, "We are blessed with the blessings of Abraham."[36] But to look at us, you certainly wouldn't have thought we were blessed. But we had gotten hold of Galatians 3:13, "Christ hath redeemed us from the curse of the law." We refused to go by what we saw on the outside.

[36]Galatians 3:13-14

Marte and I chose to go by what we saw on the inside. So we kept repeating, "God is going to make a way where there seems to be no way. This mountain of adversity will be cast into the sea. We will sail on!"

As we pulled up in front of our trailer Marte asked, "Bob, what are you going to do?"

"I'm not going to do anything," I said. "I have cast this care on the Lord, in Jesus' name!" God expects us to do all we can and then trust Him for the rest. That was what I was doing, because there was nothing more I could do. We went into our tiny 8 x 35 foot trailer, shut the door and went to bed.

The next morning I had just awakened when the Lord spoke to me in an audible voice. It was like He had been standing beside my bed waiting for me to wake up. "I'm going to send one of My ministers to change that tire for you. I don't want you to think about it."

So I put it out of my mind, but Marte asked, "What are you going to do?"

"I'm not going to do anything. The Lord said someone was coming to change the flat," I said.

At three o'clock that afternoon, a Christian brother came by our trailer and asked, "Bob, what's wrong with your truck?"

"It has a flat," I said.

"Well, I'll fix it," he said.

I had been waiting to see what the Lord would do. My friend removed the tire, and took it to a service station. However, the tire was an odd size and the service station mechanic felt it was beyond repair.

My friend told me what the mechanic had said and added, "I'm going to my dad's house in Ennis (thirty miles away), and I'll call some service stations and tire companies there to see if they have the size."

He went to Ennis, but no one had a tire that size. But, would you believe, his dad, of all people, had one that exact size in his garage. An amazing miracle! The next day he brought the tire back, and put it on the truck.

This was a giant lesson in my walk with the Lord in what He can do when we turn to Him and roll our cares upon Him.

God knows where you live and what you need. He even knows the number of hairs on your head.[37] So why let that mountain of adversity overwhelm you? Cast your cares on the Lord,[38] and believe they will be removed.

I could tell you story after story of how God has moved mountain after mountain of adversity out of our way so that we could see our dreams come to pass. Marte and I have faced every mountain imaginable. Sometimes I think there couldn't be anything else for us to face. But I am

[37]Luke 12:7   [38]I Peter 5:7

sure that if another mountain of adversity arises God will help us overcome it, because God's grace is sufficient to handle any situation.

> And he said unto me, My grace is sufficient for thee: for my strength is made perfect in weakness.   II Corinthians 12:9

Right now you may be facing some mountains, but God's grace is sufficient. When you have God's favor on your life then you can be the head and not the tail.[39] Believe it!

Believing is the only way you will ever see your dream come true. You must believe what you are saying if you expect to see it. Then follow your dream.

> Therefore I say unto you, What things soever ye desire [godly desire; the desire of your heart; your dream], when ye pray, believe that ye receive them, and ye shall have them.
>   Mark 11:24

Several years ago the Lord spoke these words to me, "Bob, believe when you pray, because it is through believing that the answer to your prayer is conceived in your spirit, and when you act on your dream you give birth to it."

Then the Lord used Marte as an example. At this time, she was pregnant. "She is pregnant now, isn't she? She has the baby now, hasn't she?" the Lord asked. I knew this was true for I had felt the baby kick. I knew we had the baby even though we had not yet seen the baby. I also knew that later we would see and hold the baby. This

[39]Deuteronomy 28:13

is the way faith works. What you believe regulates your life for success or failure. Your dream will never come to pass if you do not believe it is possible.

Declare that your dream is fulfilled. When you do this, then life's adversities will not be able to defeat you. Discouragement has destroyed the dreams of lots of people. There was a time when inspiration filled their hearts, but Satan zapped their dreams and they lost their vision. But God created you to reign with Him, not to wallow in fear at Satan's feet.

When God created Adam, He gave him the authority to decide, decree, and declare what was permitted in the earth. But Adam lost this authority when he yielded to Satan's temptation.

After Adam's fall, Satan became the god of this world.[40] But God sent Jesus, His Son, Who redeemed mankind through His death on Calvary and restored mankind's authority.

> For if by one man's offence death reigned by one; much more they which receive abundance of grace and of the gift of righteousness shall reign in life by one, Jesus Christ.
> Therefore as by the offence of one judgment came upon all men to condemnation; even so by the righteousness of one the free gift came upon all men unto justification of life.
> Romans 5:17-18

Because of this sacrifice, you can now call upon God and change your destiny. An interesting biography appears in I Chronicles 4:9-10.

[40]II Corinthians 4:4

In just two verses, a man's story is told. He was born under distressing circumstances. In fact, they were so distressing that his mother called him "Jabez" which in Hebrew means *distressed; burdened down; beat up; grieved, oppressed, depressed*. Evidently he did not have much going for him.

But the time came when Jabez wanted to break free from the distressing circumstances under which he was born; he wanted to lose the stigma of his name. So he called on the name of the Lord to deliver him. In Romans 10 it says, "Whosoever shall call upon the name of the Lord shall be saved." That can also mean, shall be delivered; shall be healed; shall be set free; shall be made whole.

> And Jabez was more honourable than his brethren: and his mother called his name Jabez, saying, Because I bare him with sorrow.
> And Jabez called on the God of Israel, saying, Oh that thou wouldest bless me indeed, and enlarge my coast, and that thou wouldest keep me from evil, that it may not grieve me! And God granted him that which he requested.   I Chronicles 4:9-10

Jabez had the faith that God could change his lot in life. Most people probably thought him foolish to even think he could change his destiny. But when Jabez called on God not only did God change his destiny, but He made Jabez successful.[41] I think this story gives us a beautiful example of someone who refused to allow the

[41]I Chronicles 4:9-10

negative circumstances of his life to get the best of him. I am convinced that if you will give God an opportunity, He will so change your life that darkness will turn into light and a burdened-down life filled with problems will be running over with blessings.

When Jesus was here on earth He maintained a position of control through words of power and authority.

> Who [meaning Jesus] being the brightness of his glory, and the express image of his person, and upholding all things by the word of his power.   Hebrews 1:3

Now He gives believers authority to restrict bad things and permit blessings through the keys of the kingdom.

> And I will give unto thee the keys of the kingdom of heaven: and whatsoever thou shalt bind [restrict from entering] on earth shall be bound [restricted] in heaven: and whatsoever thou shalt loose [permit; declare lawful] on earth shall be loosed [permitted] in heaven.
>   Matthew 16:19

These keys will give you the power to lock the devil out of your life, your home and your business.

> Not by might, nor by power, but by my spirit, saith the Lord of hosts.   Zechariah 4:6

As a believer you have the authority to declare your dream fulfilled. So declare it continually. Allow the words from your heart to give substance to your hopes.

I want you to look at two Hebrew words that are translated "declare"—*ba'ar* and *saphar*. In Deuteronomy 1:5, as Moses was declaring the law of God in great detail, he used the word *ba'ar* which has several meanings:

- To dig, as one would a well
- To dig in or engrave
- To expound
- A well

Each of these meanings carry with it the idea of digging deep, finding something valuable, and making it last over generations. When you declare your dream, it signifies that you have dug deep into your spirit and have found something valuable that will last for a long time.

The second Hebrew word, *saphar*, also has several meanings:

- To engrave on stone or on the hearts of men
- Muster master (one who calls the roll)
- To number, to count, or to take a census
- To tell, to narrate, or to announce
- A writing or a letter
- A book

Again, each of these meanings carries the implication of calling attention to something and recording it for longevity. David used *saphar* in

Psalm 2:7 when he said, "I will declare the decree." In this instance, he used the fourth meaning: to tell, narrate or announce.

When you declare your dream, you are using the same meaning. You announce your dream. Proclaim it. State it clearly. But you are also making a permanent record for longevity. Declaring a dream is no whimsical fancy that may change tomorrow. I'm talking about a serious, long-term commitment to your life's purpose.

In the early part of our ministry, we were preaching in a little tent. Every day I had to take a sledgehammer and drive the tent stakes down into the ground to keep them firm. The wind would blow the tent—like the winds of adversity blow our dreams—and would cause the stakes to work loose. Eventually, it would have pulled them out of the ground. But every day I would drive those stakes back into the ground.

Every day I declared, "You stakes, you will not come out of the ground. Wind, you will not pull my tent up in the air. You will not destroy my tent. You will not destroy my dream. You will not destroy my vision."

Declaring your dream—speaking and saying your dream based on God's Word—keeps the stakes in the ground.

Declare your dream fulfilled by speaking words of faith. Every time you speak the Word of God, it is like driving those tent stakes back into the ground. The Word works for everyone, not just for preachers. The Word is no respecter of persons, nor does it ever return void. What God will do for one, He will do for another.

Reading God's Word will cause your faith to grow strong, so doubt and fear will not invade your life. Once Jesus was asleep in the boat crossing the Sea of Galilee with His disciples.[42] A storm arose suddenly and frightened the disciples. They awakened Jesus from His sleep and He quieted the storm, but then He asked, "Where is your faith?"[43] In so many words, He was saying they could have rebuked the storm for themselves. They could have spoken words of faith.

When Satan tries to destroy your dream, stand in faith and refuse to take "no" for an answer. There may even be times when you will need to be violent in your spirit.

> And from the days of John the Baptist until the present time the kingdom of heaven has endured violent assault, and violent men seize it by force [as a precious prize]—a share in the heavenly kingdom is sought for with most ardent zeal and intense exertion.
>
> Matthew 11:12 (AMP)

If you are certain that your dream is in accordance with God's will and His timing and that it aligns with the Word of God, you may, indeed, have to seize it as a precious prize. That's what a couple from India who attended Word of Faith Family Church had to do.

[42]Mark 4:37-40   [43]Mark 4:40 (PARA)

They became convinced that God wanted them to have a house. Realizing that there is a fine line between presumption and faith, they searched the Scriptures and prayed until they verified their dream. Then they went to work decreeing and declaring it.

First, they found the house they wanted, made a $400 deposit and applied for a loan. Then they began to declare the house was theirs. In the meantime, the mortgage company called to say they needed a larger deposit and more money in the bank.

John didn't have any more money to put down on the house, nor could he increase his account. But the following Sunday while I was taking an offering for the building fund, he gave the balance of what he had as a seed-gift. "When I need money," he said, "I give money, especially when the man of God asks for it."

The next day the mortgage company asked why their bank account had gone down. John explained and then he and his wife came to the church to pray. They began to call things that were not as though they were; they continued to declare that the house was theirs. Afterwards, they drove over to the house and found workmen painting the house for someone else.

John went to the salesman, "Why is this other person's name on my property? This is my property!"

"Sir," the salesman answered, "your application for a loan was rejected because you don't have enough income. The other man has bought the property. See, here are the papers."

"He cannot live in my house," John said. "This is my house, and I'm going to live in it."

John and his family began to seize their dream as though it were a precious prize. Their faith became violent and relentless; they began to act on their faith, refusing to accept "no" as an answer.

The next Sunday I took up another offering for the building fund, and John gave again. He believed that if he put God first, God would do the miraculous.

Then he and his wife began telling all their friends, Christian and Hindu, that soon they would be moving into their new house. It was the middle of winter and things had not changed. The other man's name was still on the property title. But this did not stop John from making plans and taking all the necessary steps to move. He believed that house was his.

Finally, John got really upset with the devil and told him to get out of the house because it belonged to him and his family. He was still declaring his dream and taking his answer by force.

Shortly after this John received some miracle money, and the following week the salesman called saying, "You have won the battle. The house is yours!"

John and his wife are ordinary people with great faith in God. The Lord put a dream in their heart, and they kept that dream alive by declaring it again and again. They believed God had given them that house, so they stood on their faith and refused to give up.

Perhaps Satan has been trying to hinder the fulfillment of your dream. You don't have to take that; you can stand in faith and call forth your dream. Remember, you can change your destiny. After you decide what you want, you can decree and declare it according to the Word of God. Don't let anything or anyone stop you!

7

How Others
Followed Their Dreams

Your destination depends on what you see, but without action your dream will never become reality.

I get thousands of letters from people just like you who have stepped out in faith and have discovered that God always keeps His Word. These four families each had dreams that they submitted to the will and timing of God. They put God first in everything, charted their lives by those dreams and have discovered how exciting a God-led life can be.

Corbet and Sherry were raised in a Pentecostal Church, but they rebelled against God, choosing drugs and life in the fast lane. Corbet says, "I didn't have any use for God's way of doing things."

Then Corbet severely injured his back on the job and was unable to work. A short time later, Sherry lost her job, and the couple had to live on their workman's compensation and unemployment checks. But with Corbet's mounting doctor bills, plus the high cost of their drug habit, their money was soon gone. They were forced to go on welfare and food stamps.

Their marriage also began to deteriorate. Corbet grew depressed and suicidal because he felt their financial situation was hopeless.

"I didn't like myself very much. I thought about killing myself but never got around to it," he says.

One night Corbet and Sherry were asked to join friends in an anniversary celebration. But an innocent argument at the party turned into a nightmare when their friend began to beat his wife. Somehow Corbet managed to get both women in his car and lock the doors. But the man ran at the car and punched his fist through the window. He was aiming for his wife, but instead he hit Sherry, breaking her nose. Corbet's anger turned to hate when no legal action was taken about the attack. "I looked at what he had done to Sherry and his wife, and decided the man didn't deserve to live," he recalls.

Corbet was on his way to kill his former friend when he saw his brother who was on his way to church. After talking with him, Corbet and Sherry realized that their lifestyle was driving them to self-destruction, so in desperation, they headed for church. At the church they prayed, but left still feeling empty.

The next morning as Corbet flipped through the TV channels, he came across our *Success-N-Life* program. Quickly he switched the channel, but something made him turn back. At that particular time, I was praying for people to turn their lives over to the Lord. He asked Sherry to watch, and they both committed their lives to Jesus. They were both immediately delivered from a 10-year drug habit.

Later in the program they called in a $100 vow.

> Offer unto God thanksgiving; and pay thy vows unto the most High:
>   And call upon me in the day of trouble:
> I will deliver thee, and thou shalt glorify me.
> Psalm 50:14-15

Almost overnight, Corbet was changed; instead of anger and hate, he was filled with joy and love for God.

Faithfully, they paid their $100 vow and daily watched *Success-N-Life*. One day as I prayed for those needing healing, Corbet laid his hand on the TV screen and instantly his back was healed. Three weeks later he was back on his old job, after a 14-month absence, and able to do all the things he had done prior to his accident.

Corbet had always dreamed of opening an automobile repair shop. Then one day as he watched the program, he heard me give a word of knowledge for someone wanting to start their own business. Corbet knew this was for him, so he made a $500 vow for faith to believe for success with his dream and began paying on it.

> And [God] Who provides seed for the sower and bread for eating will also provide and multiply your [resources for] sowing and increase the fruits of your righteousness [which manifests itself in active goodness, kindness and charity].   II Corinthians 9:10 (AMP)

Sherry, also watching the program, made a $500 vow for a baby and for better transportation. Doctors had warned Sherry that, due to a blood disorder, a pregnancy could result in death for her and the child.

But they both stepped out in faith and believed God to fulfill their dreams. God has not only restored their marriage, but He has given them a healthy baby boy. Corbet has his own repair shop and they have replaced their old car with two newer vehicles.

The windows of Heaven have truly opened for this couple, and their dreams have all come true. Both Corbet and Sherry are filled with the

Holy Spirit, and are growing in the love of the Lord.

"Praise God for Robert Tilton's teaching me how to simply believe and receive whatever I need from God," Corbet says.

> Thou shalt make thy prayer unto him, and he shall hear thee, and thou shalt pay thy vows.
> Thou shalt also decree a thing, and it shall be established unto thee: and the light shall shine upon thy ways.   Job 22:27-28

Linda and her family lived behind a hospital in a 50-year-old dilapidated house that needed a complete renovation. "The roof leaked so bad that when it rained outside, it also rained inside," Linda writes.

But they didn't have the money to make the necessary repairs or to move. Although she had prayed for four years for a new house, and had faithfully given her tithes, her financial situation remained the same. Then Linda started watching my program, *Success-N-Life,* daily. She made a $100 vow for her dream house and began paying on it immediately. However, after I gave a word of knowledge to someone who wanted a new house and a new beginning, she made a second vow for $1,000. Linda felt this word of knowledge was for her.

> They that observe lying vanities forsake their own mercy.

> But I will sacrifice unto thee with the voice
> of thanksgiving; I will pay that that I have
> vowed. Salvation is of the Lord.
>
> Jonah 2:8-9

Shortly after this, she noticed that the hospital was buying up all the land around their house. So she decided to offer her property to the hospital administrators. Armed with an anointed prayer cloth, Linda met with the hospital officials and presented them with her proposal. Three days later, the sale was approved for the exact amount she had asked.

This sale gave Linda and her family enough money to buy a four-bedroom, two-bath dream house with many good features, including a roof that did not leak. She and her family are also driving "in style," after someone gave them two newer cars. Linda feels they were blessed because of her vow, and says, "Vowing is an opportunity to receive a new beginning."

Shortly after their marriage, Larry and Deborah made some financial decisions which put them heavily in debt. Even though they were saved and attending a Word Church, they could not see a solution to their financial mistake. The art of "juggling money" became second nature to them, and they often had to choose between buying food for their growing family and paying their bills. "Our lives and even our planning were completely governed by the debts we owed," says Larry.

One day, Deborah came across a TV program that she thought featured biographies of very rich people. Then a few days later after turning on the same program, she realized they were talking about Jesus! The program was *Success-N-Life*, and Larry and Deborah listened while I shared God's Word on vowing. Then they researched the scriptural references I had given on the program to be sure the interpretations were biblical.

After this they agreed to vow for a car payment that was due. The next week after sending in their $50 vow, Deborah received an unexpected bonus in her paycheck which covered their car payment!

Elated, Larry and Deborah made a $1,000 vow, asking God to help them get completely out of debt to the ten creditors that were hounding them.

> Honour the Lord with thy substance and with the firstfruits of all thine increase:
> So shall thy barns be filled with plenty, and thy presses shall burst out with new wine.
> Proverbs 3:9-10

Soon after this Larry felt led to attend our Bible school in Dallas, and this meant a major move for the family. But when Deborah asked about a transfer from her supervisor, she was told that attending Bible school was not a valid reason for an approved transfer. Disappointed but not discouraged, the couple decided to release their faith by making another vow of $500 for the fulfillment of their dream. Deborah then submitted her official request for a position in the Dallas office, giving as her reason "attending Bible school." Two days later she received an approval notice.

Larry and Deborah's faith was growing stronger and stronger, but the next mountain to be moved was the sale of their house. They had put their house on the market hoping it would sell quickly, but three months later they still did not have a prospective buyer.

During this time I had been ministering on Job 22:27-28, explaining how we can decide, decree and declare our dreams. So they made another $100 vow and paid it in full that same morning; they were believing for a buyer for the house. They felt they had the right to decree a thing and know God would establish it to them.[44]

Upon returning home from a short trip to Dallas, they found two offers on the house waiting for them. The very next day they accepted one of the offers and sold their house.

Larry and Deborah are now out of debt, and able to save a portion of their income each month. They have moved into a new home, Larry is attending Bible School, and they are actively involved in ministry at Word of Faith. Deborah has transferred to a suitable and fulfilling job here in Dallas. All their dreams are being fulfilled.

"As a result of God using you to teach us about vowing, our lives have completely

[44]Job 22-28

changed," Larry says. "We always had dreams, but now we are living many of the dreams we had in the past."

David and Christine, married for seven years, thought they had a normal amount of debts for a young couple. David had a good job as an engineer, but they never seemed to get ahead. The financial pressures that built up put their marriage under a lot of stress.

David had taken a second job to meet the needs of his expanding family, but was unhappy with the time spent away from his wife and children. "Anxiety was getting the best of me," says David, "We weren't too far behind in our bills, but I was desperate in my heart."

David had always dreamed of having his own business. He had invented a home water purifier, but he did not know how to market the idea.

Christine had never felt worthy as a person, so did not feel she was good enough to receive God's blessings. She constantly worried about David, their marriage, finances, and a pastor friend of theirs who was in debt and losing his faith.

One day, while feeding her two-month-old son, Christine turned on the TV and my *Success-N-Life* program was on. She was intrigued by my teaching on vowing. After David got home from work, she told him about the program, and the next day he came home for lunch and they watched the program together.

David knew immediately he had found the key to the success he was looking for. David recalls, "I have never been ministered to so much in one hour! I knew faith was my answer."

Christine had an urgent desire to vow $100 for their pastor's financial need, and she paid the vow with money she had saved from the change David left around the house. Several days later, their pastor received a $5,000 check! Christine was so excited about the way God had moved that she made a $500 thanksgiving vow.

David continued watching *Success-N-Life,* and as the days went by, the concept of making a vow became real to him. He made two vows totaling $950 for his business project and his financial situation.

"I mortgaged my whole future to God. All my abilities, plans and money were placed in His hands," David says.

> Give, and it shall be given unto you; good measure, pressed down, and shaken together, and running over, shall men give into your bosom. For with the same measure that ye mete withal it shall be measured to you again.
> Luke 6:38

Within two weeks of making his two vows, David's home water purifier idea was sold to a manufacturer for $7,000, and he received $23,000 for his first order with a promise for future sales. Today, David works full-time in his own business. His water purifier system is featured in the catalog of one of the largest mail order retailers in the nation, and sales continue to come in.

God's blessings are continuing in Christine's life, too. She has been set free of her feelings of unworthiness and now has the assurance of God's love. With their financial problems solved, no longer is there worry or strife in their marriage.

Now David feels called to share the message of God's abundance and prosperity with others, and he and Christine have opened up their home to show videos of *Success-N-Life* to their friends.

"This all started when we moved out of our natural ability and into God's by making that vow of faith," David says.

8

Stretch Your Faith
by Your Gift

*The world is waiting for you to burst forth
with the dream in your heart. There is
no limitation to what you can do.*

T he whole world is waiting for you to bring
forth that dream in your heart. There are
no limitations to what God will do in you,
through you, and for you.

Not long ago, as I was praying early one
morning, the presence of God flooded my prayer
closet and saturated me. Suddenly, in a vision

I saw a big warehouse full of packages. These packages were gifts—blessings, dreams, and answers to prayer available there for the asking.

I remember one item in the warehouse was something I had been desiring for a long time, but had not felt able to receive it. When I looked closer, I saw that my name was on the package and the Lord told me that it was still there waiting for me.

As I began to look around this big warehouse full of blessings, I saw names on other packages, too. These were the names of the people for whom those gifts were designated—blessings and dreams they had desired but, for some reason, never really asked for. Like me, they may have thought they didn't deserve them, or didn't see how they could receive them. So they never asked for them.

God wants to bless you—but He does that in answer to your prayers.[45] The Bibles says, "Ye have not, because ye ask not."[46] Many blessings we dream of, many victories we need, many answers we're longing for are in God's warehouse of blessings, waiting for us. Yet, because we don't see how they could come to pass, we don't ask for them. And since we don't ask, our blessings and dreams remain unclaimed.

It is through prayer that we receive from God. We need to realize that prayer is what will bring God's assistance on the scene to change things

[45]John 16:24   [46]James 4:2b

in our lives. Jesus Christ came to change things. The first miracle recorded in the Gospels was when He changed the water into wine;[47] He changed sickness into health;[48] He changed lack into abundance.[49] He is still changing things today; He can turn your dreams into realities.

What blessing are you longing for today? What desire is in your heart that maybe you've thought you weren't worthy of, and so you haven't prayed for it?

No matter what it is, God has the answer for you in His warehouse of blessings. Maybe you haven't asked because you don't feel worthy. Let me tell you something: If you belong to Jesus, you're worthy—not on the merits of your own righteousness, but on His.[50]

If you're not sure you ever accepted Jesus as your Savior, if there's no assurance in your heart that you do belong to Him, I want to encourage you to pray the prayer that follows this chapter. The Bible says, "For whosoever shall call upon the name of the Lord shall be saved."[51] Salvation is the greatest gift God has available for you in His warehouse of blessings—and it's yours for the asking.

Once you receive Jesus as your Savior, an unlimited supply of additional blessings is available to you as well. So bring your dreams, desires, anxieties, and problems to God. He has the answer to your prayers, that blessing you've been

[47]John 2:6-10 [48]Matthew 8:16 [49] Mark 6:35-44 [50]II Corinthians 5:21 [51]Romans 10:13

waiting for, that dream you so desperately want, and He is ready to deliver it to you.

But He is waiting for you to ask. Remember, "You have not, because you ask not." And Jesus said, "Ask and you will receive, and your joy will be complete."[52] Asking in faith is letting God know He is your source of supply.

By acting on your faith, you are releasing God to move through you to create, change, subdue and bring to pass the dream in your heart.

> Delight thyself also in the Lord; and he shall give thee the desires of thine heart.
>
> Psalms 37:4

One of the best ways I know of acting on your faith is to give God the best gift you can as a thanksgiving offering in advance for what you believe you receive.

> Give, and it shall be given unto you; good measure, pressed down, and shaken together, and running over, shall men give into your bosom. For with the same measure that ye mete withal it shall be measured to you again.
>
> Luke 6:38

> But this I say, He which soweth sparingly shall reap also sparingly; and he which soweth bountifully shall reap also bountifully.
>
> II Corinthians 9:6

You release God's power to give back to you through your giving. The best way to start is to give Him your best gift—of $15, $25, $50, $100 or more. Whatever amount you choose to give, make sure that it is something that will take faith

---

[52]John 16:24 (NIV)

to give. There's something about giving that releases faith.

Worship God with your vows, your tithes and your offerings. Make a vow and pay on it each week as the Lord prospers you. When you give to this worldwide evangelistic ministry, you stretch your faith beyond yourself and your abilities. You reach out to God for supernatural supply.

Decide that today is the beginning of the fulfillment of your dream by worshipping God through your giving. Decree success through your vow, and declare that it be so. Have faith in the plan God has for your life, and be confident that you are already charting your course by that dream.

Do not let others' doubt and unbelief stop you from receiving all that God has for you. Receive it first spiritually and then naturally. Many times people listen to others and look at their circumstances, then they start figuring out reasons they cannot realize their dreams. I want you to know something: You can see the fulfillment of your dreams. You can do all things through Jesus Christ[53] as you continue to align your dreams to His will and His Word.

I have faith to agree with you that every dream you decide, decree and declare is going to come to pass. I want to release God's Spirit and presence into your life, so you can receive all that Jesus bought for you at Calvary. I want

[53]Philippians 4:13

to agree with you that as you follow the dream God has placed in your heart you will find excitement, fulfillment and peace beyond your wildest imagination.

Right now, it is important for you to act upon your faith by giving God your best gift, to stretch your faith for your greatest dream to come to pass. When you help God reach His dream of carrying His Gospel around the world, He helps you reach your dream in life.

> But seek ye first the kingdom of God, and his righteousness; and all these things shall be added unto you.   Matthew 6:33

As you believe God's Word, faith will come into your heart. He wants you to yield yourself to Him and act upon that faith today. If you cannot send $100, make a vow to God that you will give Him $100. Then, today, send your best gift of $50, $35, $25, or whatever you can toward this vow; and each week do your best to pay toward it so you can have faith to receive God's best. As you honor God with your giving, get ready for your biggest dream, your greatest desire, your greatest miracle, to come to pass.

I have enclosed a special form in this book with a place for you to write down the things you have decreed and that you want me to pray about. God has given me His supernatural power and anointing so that I can minister to you. That's why I give of myself and pledge to pour out my heart in prayer for you. You are not buying my prayers; they are free. You are simply giving God a thanksgiving offering for what you believe you receive.

> You will make your prayer to Him, and He will hear you, and you will pay your vows.
> You shall also decide and decree a thing and it shall be established for you, and the light [of God's favor] shall shine upon your ways. Job 22:27-28 (AMP)

Mary, whose story I shared in the preface of this book, refused to give up, even when everything seemed to be against her. She did not look back, but she looked forward and God gave her a new direction.

"I will not let anyone or anything limit me," she said. "I will not be satisfied with being a sailboat out in the sea, drifting around. I will...chart my course in the sea of life."

You, too, can chart your course by the dreams God has placed in your heart. I have asked God to open your eyes to your dreams and to motivate you to act on them. I have shown you in this book how to select the right dream and start with it, how to plan your life, how to run with your dream, how to chart your course and decree your destiny. Now the rest is up to you. Once you follow the dream, you will take charge of your life and change your destiny. Why don't you do it now? The whole world is waiting for the dreams in your heart to burst forth.

A Word from the Lord for You

Beloved, what do you desire? What would you like Me to do for you? Oh, how I have loved you. I have looked ahead and seen the things you need, and I have already made provisions for you. The things that you need are waiting for you. So ask Me, and believe that you will receive them from Me. Ask in faith, believing, not doubting, and you will have the desires of your heart.

My dear friend, before you lay this book aside, make sure you put God first so you, too, may have the desires of your heart.

First, ask Jesus to cleanse you of your sins. You don't have to clean up your life first—God will do it for you. He will also give you a new heart, new desires, and the Spirit of truth.

If you follow these new desires—which are based on God's Word—you will have a beautiful new life on earth and eternal life.

Pray this prayer out loud and believe:

"Father in Heaven, I've heard Your Word, and I want to be born again. Jesus, cleanse me of my sins. I want to be a child of God. I want to give my life to You. Make me a new person. Be my Lord and Savior.

"I believe I'm now born again, because the Word of God says I am! Jesus is my Lord. Thank You, Jesus, for a new life. Amen."

Now, don't go by what you think or feel. Go by what God's Word says. You are saved—you are born again. Believe it!

If you prayed this prayer sincerely, then call us at our 24-hour prayer line—(214) 620-6200—and a prayer minister will help you. Or, write for more information (with no obligation):

"Salvation Information"
Robert Tilton Ministries • P. O. Box 819000 • Dallas, Texas 75381
In Canada: P.O. Box 4900 • Vancouver, BC V6B 4A6

Scriptures on Vowing

Thou shalt make thy prayer unto him, and he shall hear thee, and thou shalt pay thy vows.

Thou shalt also decree a thing, and it shall be established unto thee: and the light shall shine upon thy ways.   Job 22:27-28

Vow, and pay unto the Lord your God: let all that be round about him bring presents unto him that ought to be feared.

He shall cut off the spirit of princes: he is terrible to the kings of the earth.
Psalm 76:11-12

They that observe lying vanities forsake their own mercy.

But I will sacrifice unto thee with the voice of thanksgiving; I will pay that that I have vowed. Salvation is of the Lord.
Jonah 2:8-9

When thou vowest a vow unto God, defer not to pay it; for he hath no pleasure in fools: pay that which thou hast vowed.

Better is it that thou shouldest not vow; than that thou shouldest vow and not pay.
Ecclesiastes 4:4-5

Now he that ministereth seed to the sower both minister bread for your food, and multiply your seed sown, and increase the fruits of your righteousness.
II Corinthians 9:6-10

Scriptures on Giving

Honour the Lord with thy substance, and with the firstfruits of all thine increase:

So shall thy barns be filled with plenty, and thy presses shall burst out with new wine. Proverbs 3:9-10

Bring ye all the tithes into the storehouse, that there may be meat in mine house, and prove me now herewith, saith the Lord of hosts, if I will not open you the windows of heaven, and pour you out a blessing, that there shall not be room enough to receive it. Malachi 3:10

Give, and it shall be given unto you; good measure, pressed down, and shaken together, and running over, shall men give into your bosom. For with the same measure that ye mete withal it shall be measured to you again. Luke 6:38

He which soweth sparingly shall reap also sparingly; and he which soweth bountifully shall reap also bountifully.

Every man according as he purposeth in his heart, so let him give; not grudgingly, or of necessity: for God loveth a cheerful giver.

And God is able to make all grace [earthly blessing and favor] abound toward you; that ye, always having all sufficiency in all things, may abound to every good work:

(As it is written, He hath dispersed abroad; he hath given to the poor: his righteousness remaineth for ever.

Now he that ministereth seed to the sower both minister bread for your food, and multiply your seed sown, and increase the fruits of your righteousness.)

II Corinthians 9:6-10

When thou vowest a vow unto God, defer not to pay it; for he hath no pleasure in fools: pay that which thou hast vowed.

Better is it that thou shouldest not vow, than that thou shouldest vow and not pay.

Ecclesiastes 4:4-5

There is a sore evil which I have seen under the sun, namely riches kept for the owners thereof to their hurt.

But those riches perish by evil travail: and he begetteth a son, and there is nothing in his hand.

Ecclesiastes 5:13-14

Scriptures to Stand On

You Are Righteous in Christ
For he hath made him [Christ] to be sin for us, who knew no sin; that we might be made the righteousness of God in him.
II Corinthians 5:21

But of him are ye in Christ Jesus, who of God is made unto us wisdom, and righteousness, and sanctification, and redemption.
I Corinthians 1:30

And be found in him, not having mine own righteousness, which is of the law, but that which is through the faith of Christ, the righteousness which is of God by faith.
Philippians 3:9

Even as Abraham believed God, and it was accounted to him for righteousness. Know ye therefore that they which are of faith, the same are the children of Abraham.
Galatians 3:6-7

Even the righteousness of God which is by faith of Jesus Christ unto all and upon all them that believe: for there is no difference.
Romans 3:22

For what the law could not do, in that it was weak through the flesh, God sending his own Son in the likeness of sinful flesh, and for sin, condemned sin in the flesh: that the righteousness of the law might be fulfilled in us, who walk not after the flesh, but after the Spirit.   Romans 8:3-4

Jesus Gives You Authority
And ye shall know the truth, and the truth shall make you free. If the Son therefore shall make you free, ye shall be free indeed.
                                        John 8:32,36

Behold, I give unto you power to tread on serpents and scorpions, and over all the power of the enemy: and nothing shall by any means hurt you.
                                        Luke 10:19

And these signs shall follow them that believe; In my name shall they cast out devils; they shall speak with new tongues.
                                        Mark 16:17

And they overcame him [Satan] by the blood of the Lamb, and by the word of their testimony; and they loved not their lives unto the death.
                                        Revelation 12:11

Speak the Word

For verily I say unto you, That whosoever shall say unto this mountain, Be thou removed, and be thou cast into the sea; and shall not doubt in his heart, but shall believe that those things which he saith shall come to pass; he shall have whatsoever he saith.

Mark 11:23

And the Lord said, If ye had faith as a grain of mustard seed, ye might say unto this sycamine tree, Be thou plucked up by the root, and be thou planted in the sea; and it should obey you.

Luke 17:6

Through faith we understand that the worlds were framed by the word of God, so that things which are seen were not made of things which do appear.

Hebrews 11:3

You Can Overcome Satan

Finally, my brethren, be strong in the Lord, and in the power of his might.

Put on the whole armour of God, that ye may be able to stand against the wiles of the devil.

For we wrestle not against flesh and blood, but against principalities, against powers, against the rulers of the darkness of this world, against spiritual wickedness in high places.

Wherefore take unto you the whole armour of God, that ye may be able to withstand in the evil day, and having done all, to stand.

Stand therefore, having your loins girt about with truth, and having on the breastplate of righteousness;

And your feet shod with the preparation of the gospel of peace;

Above all, taking the shield of faith, wherewith ye shall be able to quench all the fiery darts of the wicked.

And take the helmet of salvation, and the sword of the Spirit, which is the word of God.

Ephesians 6:10-17

Submit yourselves therefore to God. Resist the devil, and he will flee from you. Draw nigh to God, and he will draw nigh to you. Cleanse your hands, ye sinners; and purify your hearts, ye double-minded.

James 4:7-8

Be sober, be vigilant; because your adversary the devil, as a roaring lion, walketh about, seeking whom he may devour:

Whom resist steadfast in the faith, knowing that the same afflictions are accomplished in your brethren that are in the world.

But the God of all grace, who hath called us unto his eternal glory by Christ Jesus, after that ye have suffered a while, make you perfect, stablish, strengthen, settle you.

I Peter 5:8-10

Surely he [God] shall deliver thee from the snare of the fowler, and from the noisome pestilence.

He shall cover thee with his feathers, and under his wings shalt thou trust: his truth shall be thy shield and buckler.

Thou shalt not be afraid for the terror by night; nor for the arrow that flieth by day;

Nor for the pestilence that walketh in darkness; nor the destruction that wasteth at noonday.

A thousand shall fall at thy side, and ten thousand at thy right hand; but it shall not come nigh thee.

Psalm 91:3-7

Your Testimony Can Be Another's Lifeline

Has God blessed you with an answer to prayer, a long-awaited blessing, a miracle deliverance in a time of crisis?

Your word of testimony can be used by God to bless and encourage untold multitudes and show someone in the same situation you were in that in Jesus there's always an answer.

Share your testimony with us. It may bring God's answer to someone else.

Mail to:
Robert Tilton Ministries ● P.O. Box 819000 ● Dallas, TX 75381
In Canada: P.O. Box 4900 ● Vancouver, BC V6B 4A6

ROBERT TILTON MINISTRIES
Miracle Prayer Requests

☐ Please pray and agree with me about the pressing needs in my life.

☐ I have given unto the work of God. I believe He will open the windows of Heaven unto me, and rebuke the devourer from my life, according to Malachi 3:10-11.

☐ My specific needs are:

_____

_____

_____

_____

_____

_____

_____

RETURN THIS FOR PRAYER

Name _____

Address _____

City _____ State _____

Zip _____ Phone (_____) _____

Robert Tilton Ministries • P.O. Box 819000 • Dallas, TX 75381
In Canada: P.O. Box 4900 • Vancouver, BC V6B 4A6

APPLICATION
W O R D   O F   F A I T H
AMERICA'S FAMILY HOME CHURCH

To become a registered active or associate member of this fellowship of home churches, simply complete this application and mail today.

> **Membership is for everyone, but to receive live broadcasts you *must* have a satellite dish.**

NAME: [   ] Middle Initial [ ]
FIRST

[   ]
LAST

NAME OF SPOUSE: [   ] Wife [ ] Husband [ ]

MAILING ADDRESS: [   ]
STREET
(or affix mailing label)

[   ] [   ] [   ]
CITY   STATE   ZIP

DAYTIME PHONE: [   ] - [   ] - [   ]

EVENING PHONE: [   ] - [   ] - [   ]

SPECIFY HOW MANY CHILDREN IN EACH AGE GROUP LIVING AT HOME:

AGES 0-5 □   6-10 □   11-15 □   16-20 □

Are you a born-again Christian? □ yes □ no □ not sure

Mail completed application to:
Word of Faith America's Family Home Church
P.O. Box 819000
Dallas, Texas 75381

IN CANADA:
P.O. Box 4900
Vancouver, BC V6B 4A6

If you desire full involvement and church covering, you may wish to become an active member. Please indicate below which type of membership you desire.

YES. ☐ Please register me as an *active member* of Word of Faith Family Home Church. I will consider Word of Faith as my church.

☐ Please register me as an *associate member*. I have local church involvement, but I do want to fellowship with you by satellite.

I will in no way utilize these church telecasts and ministry by satellite for my personal, financial, or influential gain.

From time to time, I may invite friends to fellowship with my family, but I will in no way try to exert authority over them or receive and keep personal offerings from them.

_____

Signed

_____

Date

Do you currently own a satellite dish? ☐ yes ☐ no

Do you currently own a VCR recorder? ☐ yes ☐ no

- **Word of Faith is not selling any satellite equipment,** nor does it receive commission or compensation for any sales. Active or associate members of Word of Faith Family Home Church can secure any and all satellite receiving equipment from any source they wish.

- **Word of Faith Family Church and World Outreach Center, Inc. assumes no liability** for your personal private viewing, or fellowship, or property, or equipment, or people participating as active or associate members. We simply offer a Christ-centered home church opportunity where people can gather in their homes and find fellowship around the Word of God with family and friends. Viewers are free to use these transmissions in whatever manner best meets their personal spiritual needs.

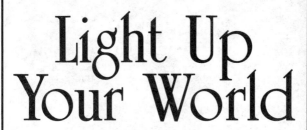

Light Up
Your World

It helps to have a person you can trust, a place you can turn to when darkness swirls around you and your family...when depression, lack and sickness threaten to overwhelm....

America's Family Home Church is just such a place, piercing the darkness and letting Jesus, the Light of the world, shine through into your life and your home.

You can dispel your darkness by becoming a part of this dynamic, Spirit-filled body of believers. Join the uplifting praise and worship and the faith-building teaching of

Sunday Morning Live
coming to you on Westar 4,
Channel 20, at 10:00 a.m. CST.

To become a member,
complete the enclosed
application and
send it to us.

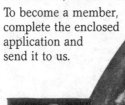